S0-BNB-875

ADVANTAGE Reading

Grade 8

Table of Contents

Table of Contents

Good Sport, Good Health

Have Fun!

CREDITS

Concept Development: Kent Publishing Services, Inc.

Written by: Linda Barr

Designer: Moonhee Pak

Production: Signature Design Group, Inc.

Art Director: Tom Cochrane

Project Director: Carolea Williams

Introduction

The Advantage Reading Series for grades 3–8 is shaped and influenced by current research findings in literacy instruction grounded in the federally mandated *No Child Left Behind Act*. It includes the following key skill strands:

- phonics/structural word analysis
- vocabulary development
- reading fluency
- reading comprehension

This series offers strong skill instruction along with motivational features in an easy-to-use format.

Take a look at all the advantages this reading series offers . . .

Phonics/Structural Word Analysis

Word analysis activities include the study of word syllabication, prefixes, suffixes, synonyms, antonyms, word roots, similes, metaphors, idioms, adjectives, adverbs, and much more. Word analysis helps students increase their **vocabulary, word-recognition skills**, and **spelling skills**.

Variety of Reading Genres

Fiction and Nonfiction

Students will have many opportunities to build reading skills by reading a variety of fiction, nonfiction, and poetry selections created in a **variety of visual formats** to simulate authentic reading styles. Each story selection builds on content vocabulary and skills introduced in the section. Fiction selections include fantasy, legends, realistic fiction, first-person narratives, and poetry. Nonfiction selections include biographies, how-to's, reports, and directions.

Graphic Information

Graphic information reading selections include charts, graphs, labels, maps, diagrams, and recipes. These types of reading opportunities help students hone **real-life reading skills**.

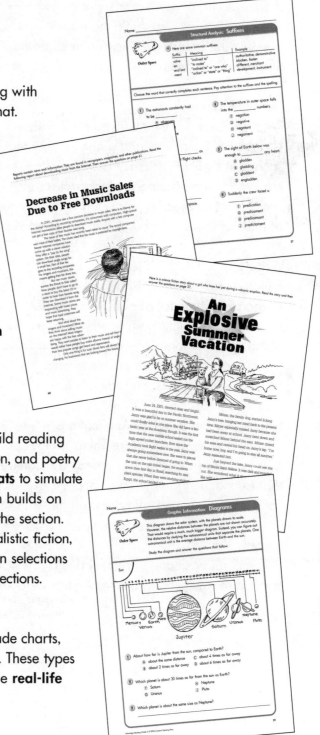

Introduction

Comprehension Strategies

Strategic comprehension activities encourage students to make connections, ask questions, make predictions, and think about strategies they can use to **increase their understanding** of the text's meaning.

Fluency Practice

Reading fluency is the ability to **read with expression,** intonation, and a natural flow that sounds like talking. Fluency is essential for comprehension because the lack of it results in choppy, robotic reading that stands in the way of making sense out of a phrase or sentence.

Writing

Reading and writing are partner skills. A **range of writing activities** helps students improve their ability to write as well as learn about different forms of writing, such as signs, notes, personal narratives, riddles, poems, descriptions, journals, stories, and friendly letters.

Extensions and Real-Life Applications

Each unit ends with a "More Things to Do" page that includes suggestions for **hands-on experiences** that extend the theme. A list of books is also included for further study and enjoyment of the unit's theme.

Answer Key

Answers for each page are provided at the back of the book to make **checking answers quick and easy.**

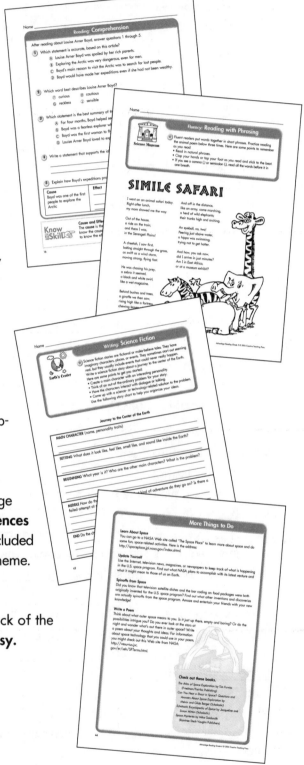

Name _____

Is It Hot Out There?

This theme focuses on the controversial issue of global warming. Many people are concerned that the burning of fossil fuels, especially coal and gasoline, is sending carbon dioxide and other gases into the air. They believe these gases are causing our atmosphere to trap more of the sun's heat, thus changing our climate. Others believe that changes in our climate are a natural part of Earth's cycle. What do you know about this topic? What do you think you know but are not sure is correct? What would you like to know so that you can better understand this issue? Complete the chart below.

What I know about global warming	_____ _____ _____ _____ _____ _____ _____
What I think I know about global warming	_____ _____ _____ _____ _____ _____ _____
What I'd like to find out about global warming	_____ _____ _____ _____ _____ _____ _____

Structural Analysis: Prefixes

Is It Hot Out There?

⭐ A **prefix** is a group of letters that is added to the beginning of a base word, also called the **root**. Prefixes change the meanings of words, so it's important to know the meanings of as many prefixes as possible. The prefixes below all relate to position, but some of them also have other meanings. For example, *para-* means "besides" but it also means "faulty or abnormal" and "almost."

Prefix	Meaning	Examples
epi-	upon	epicenter, epidermis
hypo-	under	hypodermic, hypochondria
intra-	within	intrastate, intramolecular
para-	beside	parallel, parathyroid
peri-	all around	perimeter, periodontal
super-	over and above	supervise, superimpose

Many of the answer choices below might be unfamiliar to you. Still, you can use the meaning of each prefix to choose the word that completes the sentence correctly.

1 The tissue that surrounds the heart is called the _____.
- Ⓐ pericardium
- Ⓑ intercardium
- Ⓒ extracardium
- Ⓓ supercardium

2 The _____ settles at the bottom of a fluid.
- Ⓕ paragon
- Ⓖ hypostasis
- Ⓗ peristasis
- Ⓙ epistasis

3 The new law will _____ the old one, replacing it.
- Ⓐ supersede
- Ⓑ hyposede
- Ⓒ intrasede
- Ⓓ parasede

4 A _____ is a model of excellence used for comparisons.
- Ⓕ perigon
- Ⓖ paragon
- Ⓗ hypogon
- Ⓙ extragon

5 _____ grows on other plants.
- Ⓐ A periphyte
- Ⓑ An epiphyte
- Ⓒ A paraphyte
- Ⓓ An intraphyte

6 An event that takes place between members of a population is called _____.
- Ⓕ epipopulation
- Ⓖ intrapopulation
- Ⓗ extrapopulation
- Ⓙ superpopulation

Advantage Reading Grade 8 © 2005 Creative Teaching Press

Comprehension: Idioms

Is It Hot Out There?

Idioms are phrases that do not mean exactly what they say. Over the years, these phrases have taken on a new meaning that can be confusing for anyone who is learning English. For example, when you "throw someone a curve," you do not throw a baseball. Instead, you do something unexpected that confuses or surprises the other person.

Read each sentence and the underlined idiom. Then use the meaning of the sentence to choose the correct meaning of the idiom.

1 They supported each other <u>through thick and thin</u>.
- Ⓐ no matter how their weight changed
- Ⓑ through good times and bad times
- Ⓒ through the forest and the fields
- Ⓓ together and separately

2 The football field was muddy, but both teams were <u>in the same boat</u>.
- Ⓕ soaking wet
- Ⓖ used to mud
- Ⓗ determined to win
- Ⓙ facing the same conditions

3 I tried to <u>keep a straight face</u> as the child explained her drawing.
- Ⓐ look straight at the speaker
- Ⓑ look confused
- Ⓒ look surprised
- Ⓓ not smile

4 You <u>take after</u> your brother.
- Ⓕ are shorter than
- Ⓖ follow around
- Ⓗ take care of
- Ⓙ look like

5 When the company began to <u>cut corners</u>, its sales fell.
- Ⓐ cut its prices
- Ⓑ raise its prices
- Ⓒ use cheaper materials
- Ⓓ spend more time planning

6 Don't let him <u>get the better of</u> you.
- Ⓕ get more than you do
- Ⓖ discourage you
- Ⓗ encourage you
- Ⓙ get behind you

7 He decided to <u>turn the tables</u> on the neighborhood bully.
- Ⓐ sit down at a table with
- Ⓑ trade positions with
- Ⓒ throw a table at
- Ⓓ take turns with

8 The day before our vacation, our plans <u>fell through</u>.
- Ⓕ were completed
- Ⓖ went into effect
- Ⓗ did not work out
- Ⓙ fell on the ground

Name _____

Is It Hot Out There?

Fluency: **Reading with Expression**

★ Are you concerned about global warming? Below is a speech that someone who is concerned about global warming might present to a town council. It focuses on the effect of global warming on Earth's plant and animal species. Practice reading this speech aloud, using your voice to emphasize important points. For example, you might speak louder, softer, or slower to stress key words and phrases. After reading the speech aloud at least three times, present it to a group of classmates, friends, or family members. See if you can convince them to help reduce global warming.

Are You an Endangered Species?

Do you realize that Earth has about 14 million plant and animal species? That is an enormous number of living things, right? But what would Earth be like if one million of these species suddenly disappeared? Sure, we might be able to get along without an endangered Australian tree lizard called Boyd's forest dragon and the endangered European magpie. But losing 999,998 other species would definitely make a difference! These species are all part of complex food webs, so the loss of even one can eventually result in the loss of many other species. The numbers become staggering!

What will cause these species to disappear? They will become victims of climate change. Researchers predict that by the year 2100, Earth's temperatures will rise by between 2.5 and 10 degrees Fahrenheit. This increase is already forcing some species to move to cooler areas. Species that cannot move, especially plants, are doomed!

This problem is not in the future—it's happening today. Scientists have studied 1,103 threatened species in Australia, Brazil, South Africa, and other regions. If global warming continues, by 2050—during your lifetime—between 15 and 37 percent of these species will have disappeared from Earth—forever! If this finding is applied to all species, the number of extinctions could reach one million.

What can we do in our own community? We can reduce our use of the fossil fuels that are trapping the sun's heat by walking and biking more and riding less. If we must ride, we can take the bus or carpool. We can use less fuel by buying more efficient appliances, turning up the thermostat in the summer, and turning it down in the winter. We can support laws to limit air pollution by local industries.

Humans do not own the Earth. Instead, we share it with millions of other living things. If we ruin it for them, we eventually will ruin it for ourselves. One day, pollution may cause us to become endangered ourselves!

  Advantage Reading Grade 8 © 2005 Creative Teaching Press

Comprehension: Fact and Opinion

Is It Hot Out There?

⭐ A **fact** is a statement that can be proved through research, while an **opinion** is a belief or feeling that cannot be proved. For example, it's a fact that species are disappearing from Earth, but it's an opinion that their disappearance is caused mainly by global warming. As you read, you must be able to separate facts from opinions and use facts, along with your previous knowledge, to form your own opinions.

After reading the speech on page 8, answer questions 1 through 5.

1 Choose the statement that is a fact.
- Ⓐ The Australian tree lizard is endangered.
- Ⓑ One million species will disappear by 2050.
- Ⓒ With so many species, we won't miss a few.
- Ⓓ Earth's temperatures will increase by 10 degrees.

2 Choose the statement that is an opinion.
- Ⓕ Driving a car burns fossil fuel.
- Ⓖ People are very concerned about global warming.
- Ⓗ Scientists studied 1,103 species of plants and animals.
- Ⓙ Earth has about 14 million species of plants and animals.

3 Choose the statement that is a fact.
- Ⓐ Some species cannot live in warm areas.
- Ⓑ Humans share Earth fairly with other species.
- Ⓒ Fourteen million species is an enormous number.
- Ⓓ If global warming continues, humans will become endangered.

4 Write an opinion about global warming.

_____

_____

5 Write a fact about global warming.

_____

_____

Is It Hot Out There?

Comprehension: Cause/Effect and Sequencing

⭐ As you read, you must be able to identify causes and effects. Something that makes an event happen is a **cause**, while the result of an action is an **effect**. Often an effect becomes the cause of another effect, resulting in a chain of related events. Being able to identify causes and effects helps you understand the **sequence**, or order of events, in the articles and stories you read.

After reading the speech on page 8, answer questions 1 through 5.

1 According to this speech, what is the cause of climate change?
- Ⓐ species being forced to move to cooler areas
- Ⓑ supporting laws to limit air pollution
- Ⓒ riding in buses and carpooling
- Ⓓ a rise in Earth's temperatures

2 Why does the predicted temperature rise range from 2.5 to 10 degrees?
- Ⓕ Some scientists use the Fahrenheit scale, and some use the Celsius scale.
- Ⓖ The increase is predicted for 2100, not 2050.
- Ⓗ The amount of air pollution may change.
- Ⓙ The number of lost species may change.

3 In global warming, what happens after the sun's rays reach Earth?
- Ⓐ Vehicles and industries produce air pollution.
- Ⓑ Gases from burning fossil fuels rise into the air.
- Ⓒ Gases produced by fossil fuels trap some of the heat.
- Ⓓ Gases from fossil fuels trap air pollution at Earth's surface.

4 According to this speech, what will happen if we reduce our use of fossil fuels?
- Ⓕ Extinct species will reappear.
- Ⓖ Temperatures will not rise so high.
- Ⓗ The number of species on Earth will increase.
- Ⓙ About 15 to 37 percent of species will survive.

5 Why do scientists think one million species may disappear?
- Ⓐ They have studied all 14 million species.
- Ⓑ They studied 1,103 species and made a prediction.
- Ⓒ They know some species cannot live in warm areas.
- Ⓓ They have identified one million endangered species.

Name _____

Vocabulary: **Frequently Misused Words**

Is It Hot Out There?

⭐ Some pairs of words are easily confused because they are spelled nearly alike and pronounced the same or nearly the same. However, their meanings are quite different. To decide which word in a pair of similar words is correct, you must think about the meaning of the sentence and of each word.

To practice this skill, read each sentence below and think about the meanings of the two words in parentheses. Then underline the correct word for that sentence. Use a dictionary if you need help.

1 If global warming continues, Earth might end up (baron/barren).

2 A rise in temperatures would have an (averse/adverse) effect on living things.

3 Earth's temperatures are showing an (annual/annul) rise.

4 Scientists try to (apprise/appraise) the effects of this rise.

5 We cannot take a (causal/casual) approach to this problem.

6 Human development is on a (collusion/collision) course with species survival.

7 Many animal habitats are (contagious/contiguous) with human developments.

8 Those who are working to preserve species should be (commended/commanded).

9 Some scientists (decent/descent/dissent) from the theory that Earth is warming.

10 Scientists have provided (depositions/dispositions) for both sides of this issue.

11 A thoughtful person will show (deference/difference) to both opinions.

12 (Erasable/Irascible) proponents on both sides do not help address the problem.

13 Instead of being (indigent/indignant), we need to discuss the issue calmly.

14 The air pollution problem will just (expand/expend) with time.

15 Many practical ideas may (emerge/immerge) from current discussions.

Name _____

Is It Hot Out There?

Vocabulary: Content Words

How many terms do you know that relate to global warming? Here's your opportunity to find out—and to expand your vocabulary. Fill in the bubble beside the correct answer for questions 1 through 8. If you aren't sure of an answer, look it up in a science textbook, on the Internet, or in an encyclopedia.

1 Which word refers to the specific conditions of the atmosphere at a certain place and time?
- Ⓐ climate
- Ⓑ weather
- Ⓒ climate change
- Ⓓ warm or cold front

2 What is the mixture of gases surrounding Earth?
- Ⓕ weather
- Ⓖ atmosphere
- Ⓗ carbon dioxide
- Ⓙ greenhouse gases

3 Which term describes the trapping of the sun's heat on Earth's surface?
- Ⓐ greenhouse effect
- Ⓑ greenhouse gases
- Ⓒ global warming
- Ⓓ climate change

4 What is the average weather for a particular period and time?
- Ⓕ climate change
- Ⓖ precipitation
- Ⓗ atmosphere
- Ⓙ climate

5 Which of these is NOT a fossil fuel?
- Ⓐ oil
- Ⓑ coal
- Ⓒ wood
- Ⓓ natural gas

6 Which of these is NOT a form of precipitation?
- Ⓕ sunshine
- Ⓖ snow
- Ⓗ sleet
- Ⓙ rain

7 What is the term for everything around you, including the climate and living things?
- Ⓐ greenhouse effect
- Ⓑ global warming
- Ⓒ environment
- Ⓓ atmosphere

8 The term *climate change* means _____.
- Ⓕ a change in temperatures in a certain region
- Ⓖ changes that begin with global warming
- Ⓗ changes in the amount of precipitation
- Ⓙ an exceptionally dry summer

Global Warming: What We Don't Know

First, let's define what we do know about global warming. For the most part, scientists agree that human activities, including the burning of fossil fuels, are increasing the amount of carbon dioxide and other gases in the air. Scientists also generally agree that these "greenhouse gases" trap some of the sun's heat in Earth's atmosphere. The gases form a blanket that prevents the heat from reflecting back into outer space. In this way, the gases increase the natural greenhouse effect. You might not realize that this effect is essential for our survival. It helps Earth maintain temperatures that support life. If Earth did not absorb some of the sun's heat, it would become a cold and empty place.

However, we are not sure how much these greenhouse gases will raise temperatures. Scientists have used different climate models to predict the temperature increase by the year 2100. These predictions, however, range from 2.5 to 10 degrees. This amount of variation itself makes one wonder about the accuracy of the predictions.

At the same time, bear in mind that Earth's climate has been much colder—and much warmer—than it is now. The climate in North America, for example, has ranged from the tropical temperatures that supported the dinosaurs to frigid ice ages. These changes clearly occurred without human interference. Some scientists think these ancient climate extremes were linked to changes in solar radiation or to interactions between the atmosphere and the ocean. Some believe the changes we are experiencing now are part of a natural cycle that occurs with or without us.

People are concerned about the amount of carbon dioxide in the air, but 600 million years ago, the level was twenty times higher than it is now. Humans certainly did not cause that high level of carbon dioxide back then.

Global warming might lead to melting polar caps and rising seas. It could cause both strong storms and droughts. However, we don't know how big the human role is in climate change. Many other factors might contribute, including changes in solar activity and ocean currents. We have measured Earth's temperatures with thermometers for only about 300 years. We may never be certain about temperature and climate patterns long ago. This lack of long-term data means that we cannot be sure how much more warming will occur and how fast it might happen. However, this problem definitely deserves more study.

Name _____

Reading: **Comprehension**

After you read *Global Warming: What We Don't Know*, answer questions 1 through 5.

1 Which statement best describes the author's view of global warming?

    Ⓐ It's a question that should be studied.

    Ⓑ It's a definite threat to our survival.

    Ⓒ It will lead to negative effects.

    Ⓓ It's an imaginary threat.

2 What is the main idea in this article?

    Ⓕ Earth has experienced many changes.

    Ⓖ We need to learn more about global warming.

    Ⓗ Some people are overreacting to climate changes.

    Ⓙ Scientists agree that greenhouse gases are increasing.

3 Which statement applies the ideas in this article to life in general?

    Ⓐ You should gather much information before drawing a conclusion.

    Ⓑ The study of ancient climate changes should be encouraged.

    Ⓒ People must reduce their use of fossil fuels.

    Ⓓ Scientists keep changing their minds.

4 Why does the author mention ancient climate changes?

_____

_____

5 Choose the sentence that draws a correct conclusion.

    Ⓐ We should prepare for significant global warming.

    Ⓑ We should ignore warnings about global warming.

    Ⓒ Human activities have no effect on global warming.

    Ⓓ The beneficial greenhouse effect could become harmful.

Know the **Skill**

Draw Conclusions
To draw a conclusion, you combine information from your reading with your own knowledge and experience. Then you reach a decision or form an opinion about something in the selection, something the author hinted at but did not state directly.

          Advantage Reading Grade 8 © 2005 Creative Teaching Press

Finding Fingerprints

The Union of Concerned Scientists has identified what it calls the "fingerprints" of global warming. These four trends indicate a long-term warming and may signal a significant climate change. These trends are global. But here are some ways that these fingerprints apply to the United States.

Heat waves and periods of unusually warm weather

For example, in the summer of 1998, Texas, Florida, and other states experienced a heat wave that killed more than 100 people. Temperatures in Dallas exceeded 100°F for 15 days in a row. In July 1999, the eastern half of the nation suffered a heat wave that cost 250 lives. Temperatures in Chicago reached 119°F.

Ocean warming, sea levels rising, and coastal flooding

The oceans have risen 4 to 10 inches during the past century. A further increase of 6 to 36 inches is predicted for the next century. About 50 to 100 feet of beach disappears for every foot that the oceans rise. The sea is rising at the Chesapeake Bay three times faster than the historical rate.

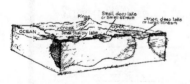

Glaciers melting

During the past 150 years, most mountain glaciers have been shrinking. They will be gone by 2100. All the glaciers in Glacier National Park in Montana will be gone by 2070 if they continue to melt at their current rate. These glaciers used to contribute much of the water used for irrigation and power in mountain areas.

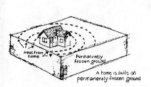

Arctic and Antarctic warming

Permafrost is a layer of frozen soil below Earth's surface. This layer, frozen for many centuries, has been melting in Arctic and Antarctic regions. This melting has forced the reconstruction of roads, airports, and buildings. In parts of Alaska, this thawing has caused the ground to sink 16 to 33 feet. In addition, the area of the Arctic Ocean covered by ice has shrunk six percent since 1978.

Just as your fingerprints can identify you, these fingerprints identify a trend that worries many scientists and others.

Reading: **Comprehension**

After reading *Finding Fingerprints*, answer questions 1 through 5.

1 Fingerprints are to global warming as robins are to _____.

    Ⓐ birds

    Ⓑ spring

    Ⓒ worms

    Ⓓ the greenhouse effect

2 *Permafrost* is often defined as "a layer of permanently frozen soil." Why is that definition inaccurate?

_____

_____

3 Which statement is a fact?

    Ⓐ Alaska is sinking.

    Ⓑ The seas are slowly rising.

    Ⓒ A heat wave is a sure sign of global warming.

    Ⓓ People who ignore global warming are being foolish.

4 The ice in the Arctic Ocean now covers six percent less area. What does this mean?

_____

5 Which generalization makes sense, based on this article?

    Ⓐ We should pay more attention to scientists' predictions.

    Ⓑ Any warming is an indication of climate change.

    Ⓒ Only these four trends indicate global warming.

    Ⓓ Small changes can indicate a major change.

Make Generalizations

When you make a generalization, you gather information, draw a conclusion, and then apply that conclusion to life in general. Next, you must evaluate your generalization to see if it is valid and makes sense. For example, you might need to add a limiting word, such as *some*, *many*, or *usually*.

A fable is a very short story, often with animal characters. It ends with a lesson or moral to guide readers in their lives. Many of the fables we read today were written long ago by a man named Aesop, who was probably a Greek slave in the sixth century B.C. At the same time, it's possible that there never was a man named Aesop, and these stories were written by someone else or even by several people.

Read *The North Wind and the Sun* and then answer the questions on page 18.

The North Wind and the Sun
by Aesop

The North Wind and the Sun disputed as to which was the most powerful, and agreed that he should be declared the victor who could first strip a wayfaring man of his clothes.

The North Wind first tried his power and blew with all his might, but the keener his blasts, the closer the Traveler wrapped his cloak around him, until at last, resigning all hope of victory, the Wind called upon the Sun to see what he could do.

The Sun suddenly shone out with all his warmth. The Traveler no sooner felt his genial rays than he took off one garment after another, and at last, fairly overcome with heat, undressed and bathed in a stream that lay in his path.

Persuasion is better than Force.

Name _____

Reading: **Comprehension**

After reading the selection *The North Wind and the Sun*, answer questions 1 through 5.

1 Which literary technique is the basis of this fable?

    Ⓐ giving inanimate things human qualities

    Ⓑ using several words with the same first sound

    Ⓒ comparing unlike things using the words *like* or *as*

    Ⓓ comparing unlike things without the words *like* or *as*

2 Would this traveler's experience be a sign of global warming? Explain your answer.

_____

_____

3 When Aesop wrote "the keener his blasts…," what did he mean?

    Ⓐ the colder the wind

    Ⓑ the warmer the wind

    Ⓒ the smarter the wind

    Ⓓ the more eager the wind

4 Why do some people use force instead of persuasion?

_____

_____

5 How would the moral of this fable guide readers in their lives?

    Ⓐ They would try the easiest solution first.

    Ⓑ They would offer bribes before threats.

    Ⓒ They would not bath in streams.

    Ⓓ They would dress in layers.

Extend Meaning
Fables offer a lesson you can apply to your own life and daily activities. For example, perhaps you know someone who attempts to control others through threats or intimidation. This fable reminds us that people are more likely to do something if doing it meets their own needs.

Advantage Reading Grade 8 © 2005 Creative Teaching Press

Name _____

Graphic Information: Bar Graphs

Is It Hot Out There?

⭐ A graph can often illustrate a trend more clearly than many paragraphs of words. These two bar graphs are based on the Common Sense Climate Index. This index combines several climate indicators, such as the frequency of extreme temperatures and record highs and lows, to show changes from normal. When a bar extends above the annual climate index (the straight line), the climate is warmer than usual. When a bar dips below the annual climate index, the climate is cooler than usual. If the bar extends 1 unit above or below the index and remains there, most people living in that region should notice the difference.

Study these two graphs and then answer the questions on page 20.

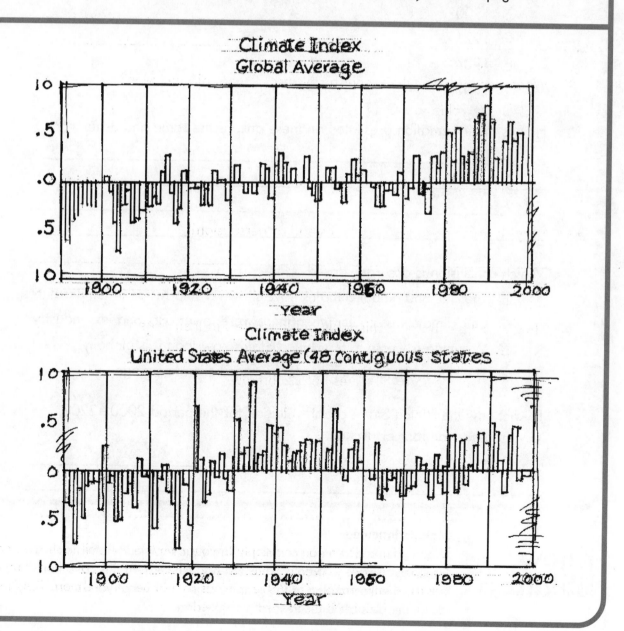

Climate Index
Global Average

Climate Index
United States Average (48 Contiguous States

Name _____

Study the graphs on page 19 and then answer questions 1 through 5.

1 What does 0 represent in the index?

　Ⓐ 0 degrees Fahrenheit

　Ⓑ the average climate

　Ⓒ 0 degrees Celsius

　Ⓓ no change

2 According to the United States graph, what was our warmest year so far?

　Ⓕ 1900

　Ⓖ 1921

　Ⓗ 1934

　Ⓙ 1953

3 How is the information presented on these graphs the same and different?

_____

_____

_____

_____

4 Which conclusion is accurate, based on the graphs?

　Ⓕ The U.S. and global climates have shown a steady rise in temperatures.

　Ⓖ Our climate was cooler when there were fewer cars and less industry.

　Ⓗ Warming is worse in the United States now than it is globally.

　Ⓙ The United States is headed for a record climate change.

5 Predict how the United States graph will look for the period 2000–2200. Give reasons for your prediction.

_____

_____

Make a Prediction
When you predict an outcome, you use your knowledge of what has happened before to predict what will happen next. In this case, you will use the information in the graphs, along with what you know about people's attitudes toward global warming.

Name _____

**Is It Hot
Out There?**

Writing: Myth

Many myths were created long ago and passed from generation to generation, usually by word of mouth. Myths often were developed to explain natural phenomena, such as the sun "rising" in the east and the seasons changing. Myths were also written to explain the unusual traits of animals, such as the hummingbird's slender beak or the lion's mane.

In myths, the characters are usually simple and may be personifications of natural forces, such as the North Wind and the Sun. The conflict is simple and clear. The setting might simply be "long ago."

Write a myth that relates to global warming and the environment. For example, you might "explain" why the weather is changing or why these changes are important. As you plan your myth:
- Choose a natural (or human-caused) event or trend and decide how you will "explain" it.
- Choose one or two characters, who might be animals or natural forces.
- Think of one or two situations the characters will face to show how this event or trend came to be.

This graphic organizer can help you plan your myth. Don't forget to give your myth an interesting title.

Natural (or unnatural) event:
Characters:
Situations the characters will face:
Solution:

Is It Hot Out There?

Writing: Myth

Write the first draft of your myth below, using the notes from your graphic organizer on page 21. Continue your story on another sheet of paper, if needed.

Then show your first draft to a partner, friend, or family member. Ask this person to explain how you could make your story clearer and more interesting. What should you add, and what should you leave out? Do the characters' actions and comments make sense? Does the story explain the event or trend you chose?

_____

_____

_____

_____

_____

_____

_____

_____

_____

_____

_____

_____

_____

_____

_____

Name _____

**Is It Hot
Out There?**

Now write the final draft of your myth, adding illustrations, if
you wish.

_____

_____

_____

_____

_____

_____

_____

_____

_____

_____

_____

_____

_____

_____

Learn More about Global Warming

The Environmental Protection Agency (EPA) sponsors an interesting Web site for young people that clearly explains many aspects of global warming, using diagrams and animation. To reach the site, use this search phrase in your Web browser: *EPA Kids Site*. You can move from this site to the EPA Global Warming Home Site for more detailed information.

You can also gather information about global warming at the *USA Today* Web site. Go to *www.usatoday.com* and click on "Weather." Then go to "Resources" and "Climate Change Science." You will find a list of links to valuable Web sites, many of them sponsored by government agencies, such as NOAA and NASA.

Climate and Health

Some diseases and parasites are present only in certain climates, but they might spread as our climate changes. Find out how global warming and climate change might affect human health. This Web site, sponsored by the U.S. Global Change Research Program, provides excellent links to studies and other sources: *www.usgcrp.gov/usgcrp/nacc/health/default.htm*.

Climate Interviews

Find out if people in your community have climate change. Interview people who have your area for ten years or longer. You might questions such as these:

- Do you spend more or less time outdoors than you did ten or more years ago? Wh
- How do you think the weather during ou years or longer ago? How do the winters
- Does the first frost in the fall seem to cor last frost in the spring?
- Do we have droughts more often or less

After you have gathered as many response can determine a pattern. Do people in your community perceive a change in your climate?

Check out these books.

Global Warming by Kathiann M. Kowalski (Benchmark Books)

Global Warming by Alvin Silverstein, Virginia Silverstein, and Laura Silverstein Nunn (Twenty-First Century Books)

Human Impact by Carole Garbuny Vogel (Franklin Watts).

Our Warming Planet by Lim Cheng Puay (Raintree)

Name _____

Revolution

The American Revolution certainly was a turning point for what is now the United States. People had to decide how important independence was to them—and whether they were willing to give their lives for it. After the war was over, they were no longer a colony of the British Empire: they were a young nation, proud and strong. What words come to your mind when you think about the American Revolution? To begin to focus on this theme, complete the word web below.

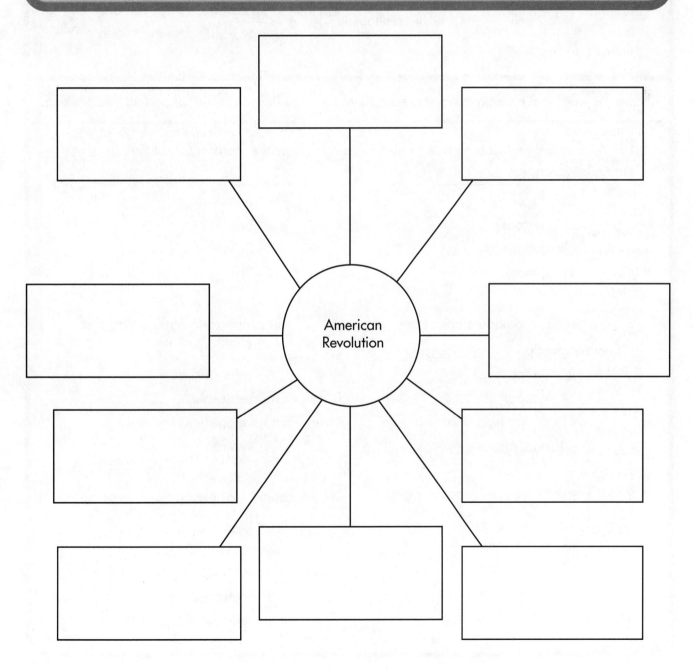

Name _____

Revolution

⭐ **Suffixes** are letters added to the ends of words that can change the meaning of the word or its part of speech. A number of suffixes change words to mean "relating to." For example, if we add the suffix -ic to the noun *history*, it becomes the adjective *historic*, meaning "relating to history." Notice the spelling change, too. Here are several suffixes that mean "relating to," along with some examples of their use:

Suffix	Examples	Suffix	Examples
-an	American, urban	-ial/ian	commercial, barbarian
-esque	Romanesque, statuesque	-ic/ical	comic, economical
-etic	athletic, alphabetic	-ish	foolish, childish

Choose the word that correctly completes each sentence. Pay attention to the suffixes and the spellings.

1 A question that doesn't need to be answered is _____.
- Ⓐ rhetorical
- Ⓑ rhetorish
- Ⓒ rhetorian
- Ⓓ rhetoric

2 Someone who understands how others feel is _____.
- Ⓕ sympathical
- Ⓖ sympathetic
- Ⓗ sympathian
- Ⓙ sympathic

3 A scene that deserves to be framed is _____.
- Ⓐ picturish
- Ⓑ picturetic
- Ⓒ picturetical
- Ⓓ picturesque

4 Someone born in Great Britain is _____.
- Ⓕ British
- Ⓖ Britian
- Ⓗ Britan
- Ⓙ Britic

5 A person who served in a war is a _____.
- Ⓐ veterinarian
- Ⓑ veterish
- Ⓒ veterian
- Ⓓ veteran

6 A course that remedies an academic problem is _____.
- Ⓕ remedetic
- Ⓖ remedian
- Ⓗ remedial
- Ⓙ remedic

Advantage Reading Grade 8 © 2005 Creative Teaching Press

Vocabulary: **Transitional Words**

Revolution

⭐ **Transitional words** are the glue that holds your writing together. They show how your ideas fit together, making your writing easier to understand. In the example below, the transitional word *because* signals that the second part of the sentence will explain the reason for the first part.

We had to be there early, because we had everyone's tickets.

Look at the categories of transitional words in the box. Choose the transitional word or phrase that belongs on each blank line. Think carefully about how the ideas are related. In some cases, more than one transitional word or phrase could be used.

Time:	first, later, then, next, after, always, now, until
Contrast:	however, but, nevertheless, despite, still, although, yet
Addition:	also, too, in addition, likewise, more, another, similarly
Explanation:	because, so, therefore, consequently, resulting from
Illustration:	for example, such as, just as, like, for instance

1 Our supervisor is very particular. _____, she wants us to sign in five minutes before our shift starts.

2 The army had been traveling on foot for days. _____, the soldiers' spirits were high.

3 My sister has applied to several colleges, _____ she hopes to be accepted by the same one our cousin attends.

4 The school just opened this year. _____ everyone is still learning where things are.

5 My neighbor teaches art classes at the local college. _____, she gives lessons in her studio at home.

6 Read over your first draft to check its organization. _____ you can make any necessary changes.

7 Sarah wanted to hear the results of the track meet _____ her friend was running.

8 During the American Revolution, many soldiers had to provide their own uniforms. _____ the government provides all the soldiers' supplies.

Fluency: **Reading with Expression**

Revolution

⭐ In 1776, the Colonies declared itself independent of Great Britain, but the British king was not about to lose one of his most profitable colonies. A patriot named Thomas Paine helped inspire Americans to fight for their freedom with a series of essays titled, *The Crisis*. General George Washington read these essays and was moved by them. He ordered that the first essay be read aloud to his troops at Valley Forge. It was Christmas Eve, and his freezing, starving soldiers were about to cross the Delaware River and confront the British troops.

Below is the first paragraph of this essay. Read it aloud, using your voice to inspire the troops with your patriotism and determination. Choose important points to emphasize with a louder voice or a slower reading rate. Practice reading the appeal at least three times. Then read it aloud, with feeling, to a member of your family.

The Crisis

THESE are the times that try men's souls. The summer soldier and the sunshine patriot will, in this crisis, shrink from the service of their country; but he that stands by it now, deserves the love and thanks of man and woman. Tyranny, like hell, is not easily conquered; yet we have this consolation with us, that the harder the conflict, the more glorious the triumph. What we obtain too cheap, we esteem too lightly: it is dearness only that gives every thing its value. Heaven knows how to put a proper price upon its goods; and it would be strange indeed if so celestial an article as FREEDOM should not be highly rated. Britain, with an army to enforce her tyranny, has declared that she has a right (not only to TAX) but "to BIND us in ALL CASES WHATSOEVER" and if being bound in that manner, is not slavery, then is there not such a thing as slavery upon earth.

Comprehension: Draw Conclusions

Revolution

To draw a conclusion, you combine information from your reading with your own knowledge and experience. Then you reach a decision or form an opinion about something in the selection, something the author hinted at but did not state directly. This exercise will help you practice drawing conclusions. First, read the excerpt from Thomas Paine's essay on page 28, and then answer questions 1 through 5.

1 Choose the sentence that draws a correct conclusion.
   Ⓐ Thomas Paine was a soldier at Valley Forge.
   Ⓑ Washington agreed with Paine's reasons to fight the war.
   Ⓒ This essay convinced Washington to cross the Delaware.
   Ⓓ Paine had second thoughts about going to war against the British.

2 Paine mentions the "summer soldier and the sunshine patriot." What did he mean by these terms?

_____

_____

3 Choose the sentence that draws a correct conclusion about Paine's beliefs.
   Ⓐ Freedom is worth making sacrifices.
   Ⓑ America will easily win its freedom.
   Ⓒ America is unlikely to win its freedom.
   Ⓓ Every American is willing to make sacrifices.

4 Paine knew that the new nation's fight for freedom would be costly. What information from the essay supports this conclusion?

_____

_____

5 Choose the sentence that draws a correct conclusion about Paine's beliefs.
   Ⓐ Taxing people does not mean keeping them in slavery.
   Ⓑ Fighting for freedom helps us appreciate it.
   Ⓒ Freedom can be bought, but it's expensive.
   Ⓓ Freedom is too highly rated.

Comprehension: **Analogies**

Revolution

⭐ Analogies test your understanding of the relationships between words. An **analogy** consists of a pair of words, followed by a single word. You must figure out how the pair of words is related and then choose a word that is related to the single word in the same way, forming a second pair of words. For example:

Barter is to *ancient cultures* as *money* is to _____.

Ancient cultures used barter or trading to get what they wanted; today most of us use money. This analogy should be completed with a term that tells who uses money, such as *modern societies*. Analogies might also involve other relationships, such as synonyms, antonyms, or cause-effect relationships.

Study the analogies below. Figure out how the first pair of words are related in the essay on page 28, and then choose the correct word to complete the second pair.

1 *Hard* is to *conflict* as *glorious* is to _____.

- Ⓐ revolution
- Ⓑ triumph
- Ⓒ soldier
- Ⓓ patriot

4 *Dog* is to *wings* as *summer soldier* is to _____.

- Ⓕ commitment
- Ⓖ sunshine
- Ⓗ vacation
- Ⓙ uniform

2 *Ostrich* is to *bird* as *taxation* is to _____.

- Ⓕ government
- Ⓖ flamingo
- Ⓗ slavery
- Ⓙ money

5 *Loyal* is to *patriotic* as *dear* is to _____.

- Ⓐ freedom
- Ⓑ precious
- Ⓒ goods
- Ⓓ cheap

3 *Defend* is to *protect* as *bind* is to _____.

- Ⓐ fight
- Ⓑ revolt
- Ⓒ bound
- Ⓓ control

6 *King* is to *leader* as *tyranny* is to _____.

- Ⓕ government
- Ⓖ democracy
- Ⓗ kingdom
- Ⓙ soldiers

Vocabulary: Frequently Misused Words

Revolution

⭐ Some pairs or groups of words are so similar that they are often confused and used incorrectly. Some of these word pairs sound nearly alike but have different meanings, while others are pronounced differently but have meanings that are easily confused. You must be familiar with the meanings of these word pairs to determine which word to use.

Read each sentence and think about the meanings of the words in parentheses. Then underline the correct word for that sentence.

1 The doctor is still not sure what (ales/ails) him.

2 The second half of the movie was actually (boaring/boring).

3 After the avalanche, the road was blocked by a (boulder/bolder).

4 The dry leaves were (born/borne) by the wind into the doorway.

5 The lookout climbed up into the highest (bow/bough) of the tree.

6 The nervous rider led his horse by its (bridle/bridal).

7 You would be wise not to (broach/brooch) that subject tonight.

8 He was a (callous/callus) and calculating leader.

9 The police officers made a careful (canvas/canvass) of the neighborhood.

10 Some societies are separated into (casts/castes).

11 One group wants to (sensor/censor) certain television programs.

12 The movie was made into a (cereal/serial) for television.

13 Which (coarse/course) did you decide to take?

14 She joined the Army (Core/Corps) of Engineers.

15 The boat dropped him off on a deserted (eyelet/islet).

Name _____

Vocabulary: Content Words

Revolution

Do you know the difference between a monarchy and a monopoly? Here is an opportunity to test your vocabulary relating to the American Revolution. Fill in the correct answer for questions 1 through 8. If you aren't sure of an answer, look it up in a social studies textbook, on the Internet, or in an encyclopedia.

1 What is a government in which the head of state is a hereditary position?
- Ⓐ monarchy
- Ⓑ monopoly
- Ⓒ socialism
- Ⓓ anarchy

2 What is a contract that requires one person to work for another person for a certain length of time?
- Ⓕ independence
- Ⓖ investment
- Ⓗ integration
- Ⓙ indenture

3 What is a group of people living in a new territory who are governed by their homeland?
- Ⓐ monarchy
- Ⓑ republic
- Ⓒ empire
- Ⓓ colony

4 Which word describes something that cannot be taken away?
- Ⓕ executive
- Ⓖ inalienable
- Ⓗ transferable
- Ⓙ representative

5 When you refuse to buy certain products, you conduct a _____.
- Ⓐ referendum
- Ⓑ secession
- Ⓒ boycott
- Ⓓ revolt

6 What is another word for taxes?
- Ⓕ representation
- Ⓖ ratification
- Ⓗ regulation
- Ⓙ revenue

7 When you give someone permission to do something, you _____ to it.
- Ⓐ object
- Ⓑ secede
- Ⓒ dissent
- Ⓓ consent

8 An introduction to a speech or document is called _____.
- Ⓕ an index
- Ⓖ a preamble
- Ⓗ an epilogue
- Ⓙ a table of contents

Advantage Reading Grade 8 © 2005 Creative Teaching Press

Read the biography, *The Common Sense of Thomas Paine*, and then answer the questions on pages 35 and 36.

The Common Sense of Thomas Paine

Born in England in 1737, Thomas Paine had a less-than-impressive start in life. First, he dropped out of school and later had trouble holding a job. While he was in London in 1774, he happened to meet Benjamin Franklin. Franklin convinced him to emigrate to the American colonies and try his luck there.

Settling in Philadelphia, Paine decided to pursue a career in journalism. He wrote about issues that concerned him and, it turned out, concerned many other colonists. One of his first essays, published in the spring of 1775, was titled, *African Slavery in America*. Paine pointed out that slavery was unjust, a view that not everyone shared at the time.

By April 1775, the colonists had begun their struggle to escape British rule. They were battling British troops at Lexington and Concord. Paine sensed the rising tension and frustration. In January 1776, he wrote *Common Sense*. More than 500,000 copies were printed and sold. As colonists read it again and again, they debated Paine's main point: that the colonies should fight for their freedom from Great Britain. Paine argued that independence must come, sooner or later.

To him, the reasons to separate from England were based on simple facts and common sense. Government was a necessary evil, he wrote, but its form had to be a democracy, not a monarchy. Paine's essay greatly influenced the wording of the Declaration of Independence. It was written and signed six months after *Common Sense* was published.

Paine joined the Continental Army himself but was not destined to be a soldier. However, his essays had an enormous impact on the Revolution, inspiring the army's soldiers and leaders. In December 1776, Paine began to write a series of pamphlets that he titled, *The Crisis*. On page 28, you read the beginning paragraph of his first pamphlet. Remember that General Washington had it read aloud to his troops just before they crossed the Delaware River.

During the Revolution, more people read Paine's pamphlets than watch the Super Bowl today. Paine donated the money he earned from the sale of the pamphlets to help finance the revolution.

Soon after the new nation was established, Paine became Secretary of the Committee of Foreign Affairs. However, only two years later he had to resign because he had disclosed secret information.

Then Paine worked for the Pennsylvania Assembly for the next nine years while he explored his interests in invention and engineering. Paine designed an iron bridge but could not convince anyone to build it. In 1787, he traveled to Europe, looking for someone to fund his bridge. There, Paine became involved in the French Revolution. He continued to write essays, this time in defense of the French Revolution. In 1793, he was arrested for not approving the execution of the French King, Louis XVI. Paine spent a year in a French jail. He begged his friends in Washington for help, but they claimed he was not an American citizen. It seems that Paine's controversial views on government and religion did not sit well with the current American leaders.

After Paine was released from prison, he stayed in France until 1802. Then Thomas Jefferson invited him to return to America. Although Jefferson admired Paine, some Americans thought he had somehow betrayed their new nation. Others were put off by his religious views. Many had already forgotten the great influence of his writing on the American Revolution.

Paine died alone in 1809 in New York City. He was a penniless alcoholic. His newspaper obituary said, "He had lived long, did some good and much harm." Today most people are grateful for his inspiring words during our revolution and wonder what harm he did.

Reading: **Comprehension**

After reading the biography on pages 33 and 34, answer questions 1 through 9.

1 Rev. Martin Luther King Jr. was to peace as Thomas Paine was to _____ .

    Ⓐ essays

    Ⓑ history

    Ⓒ integration

    Ⓓ controversy

2 Is it accurate to describe Thomas Paine as a man of many talents? Explain your answer.

_____

_____

3 What did Paine write about first?

    Ⓐ the importance of democracy

    Ⓑ American independence

    Ⓒ the injustice of slavery

    Ⓓ the French Revolution

4 More than 500,000 copies of *Common Sense* were sold. Why was this number more significant back then than it would be now?

_____

_____

5 Choose the conclusion that can be made, based on this biography.

    Ⓐ Paine has always been admired for his essays.

    Ⓑ Paine sacrificed much to support his nation.

    Ⓒ Paine had a special ability to inspire others.

    Ⓓ Paine was drawn to revolutions.

Reading: **Comprehension**

6 Why did Paine die poor and alone?

_____

_____

7 Choose the statement that is a fact.

   Ⓐ   Paine's lonely death was his own fault.

   Ⓑ   Paine did some good and much harm.

   Ⓒ   Paine was a controversial figure.

   Ⓓ   Paine was too opinionated.

8 If Thomas Paine were writing today, how much effect do you think he would have on public opinion? Would people pore over his essays, as they did back then? Explain your answer.

_____

_____

_____

9 The author writes that Paine's controversial views did not sit well with the American leaders. What does the phrase _did not sit well_ mean?

   Ⓐ   slouched

   Ⓑ   could not sit still

   Ⓒ   were too impatient

   Ⓓ   were not acceptable

Know the Skill

Idioms
An **idiom** is a group of words that does not mean exactly what it says. For example, if you finally _catch on_ to a joke, you don't actually grab the joke with your hand. You understand it. Idioms make our language more colorful, but they also make it more difficult to learn.

Historical fiction is a realistic story set in the past. Many details in the story are factual, such as information about clothing and food preparation, but the characters are fictional. The setting (time and place) usually has a major influence on the plot.

Read *After the Ride*, and then answer the questions on page 38.

After the Ride

Most mornings, Elizabeth didn't mind milking the cows, even when it was still dark out, like this April morning. Today, though, she was tired. She hadn't been able to get back to sleep after the neighbor's boy, Luke, had ridden into their barnyard hours ago and shouted so loud that the owls started hooting.

"The British are coming!" Luke had screamed. "The rider just came through and told us! We're going to stop them at the Lexington Green!"

Elizabeth yawned as she pulled open the barn door. Her lantern threw shadows on the cows as they raised their heads to moo at her. She carried her bucket over to the first one, sat on her stool, and started milking.

After Luke woke them, Elizabeth had wanted to gallop off to Lexington with her father and brother Jeb, but it was no place for a girl, her dad had firmly announced.

Suddenly she glimpsed a shadowy man standing in the door of the barn! Frantic, Elizabeth searched around her for something she could use as a weapon.

"Ma'am, please don't be frightened," the man whispered as he came closer.

Maybe she could reach the pitchfork before he caught her!

"Ma'am, could I please have some water?" he asked in a hoarse voice.

Now Elizabeth could see the man's face in the lantern light. With his worn clothes, he surely was not a British soldier. He looked tired, as if he had been riding all night, but he also looked kind. She stopped searching for a weapon.

"You can use the pump outside the barn," she told him. "But don't you know the British are coming? Shouldn't you be in Lexington with the other men?" Then a frightening thought struck her. "You...you aren't a loyalist, are you?"

He smiled and shook his head as he headed for the pump. She followed him, but not too close, just in case. After a long drink, he said, "Thanks for the water, Ma'am, and I do know the British are coming." He smiled again and headed toward Lexington.

Late the next day, Elizabeth's father and Jeb returned, worn out but full of tales about the battle. Jeb told her how a British patrol had caught Paul Revere at the end of his ride through the countryside. They had held him for a while and then let him go, but without his horse. Jeb saw him walk into Lexington just as the first shot was fired.

Suddenly Elizabeth knew who had stopped for water. She grinned as she told Jeb that she, too, had a role in the colonists' first battle for freedom!

Name _____

Reading: Comprehension

After reading *After the Ride* on page 37, answer questions 1 through 5.

1 Elizabeth worried that the stranger in the barn was a loyalist. Why was she concerned?

   Ⓐ He might be helping the colonies fight for freedom.

   Ⓑ He might be looking for her father and brother.

   Ⓒ He might support the British king.

   Ⓓ He might be a British soldier.

2 Paul Revere was a leader of the patriots, so why didn't Elizabeth recognize him?

   Ⓕ He wasn't wearing his uniform.

   Ⓖ She had not seen him before.

   Ⓗ She was too frightened.

   Ⓙ It was dark in the barn.

3 Why was Paul Revere fortunate to be walking to Lexington?

_____

_____

_____

4 Which word BEST describes Elizabeth?

   Ⓕ timid   Ⓗ aggressive

   Ⓖ patriotic   Ⓙ frightened

5 Summarize this story in one or two sentences.

_____

_____

_____

_____

Summarize
When you summarize, you share only the most important points or events in a reading selection. Usually, you present these points in the same order as they were in the selection.

            Advantage Reading Grade 8 © 2005 Creative Teaching Press

Graphic Information: Maps

Revolution

⭐ The map below traces Paul Revere's famous ride on the night of April 18, 1775 to alert the colonists that the British troops were coming. Revere began his trip at Boston and rowed across the Charles River to Charlestown. Then he rode a horse through Medford to Lexington. There he was joined by a second rider, William Dawes, who also had ridden out from Boston to warn others about the British troops. However, Dawes took a different route, which you can see on the map.

Dr. Samuel Prescott joined Revere and Dawes in Lexington, and the three men headed for Concord, where the patriots had a large store of weapons that they wanted to protect. However, a British patrol caught Revere and Dawes on the way to Concord, while Prescott escaped and rode on to Concord to warn the people there. Soon after, Dawes also escaped. Revere told the British soldiers that hundreds of patriots were waiting for them at Concord, which was an exaggeration. The troops, now eager to get to Concord, let Revere go. Revere walked back to Lexington. At Lexington, the patriots stopped the British troops, who had landed at Boston Harbor and were heading for Concord.

Study the map and then answer the questions on page 40.

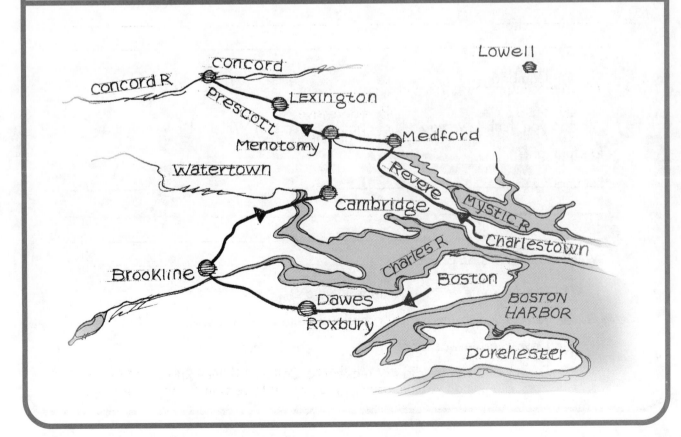

Reading: **Comprehension**

After reading the information and studying the map on page 39, answer questions 1 through 5.

1 Whose route is NOT shown on the map?

    Ⓐ Paul Revere

    Ⓑ British soldiers

    Ⓒ William Dawes

    Ⓓ Samuel Prescott

2 Compare and contrast the roles of Paul Revere and William Dawes.

_____

_____

_____

3 That night, where did Revere and Dawes meet before they reached Lexington?

    Ⓐ Concord

    Ⓑ Medford

    Ⓒ Menotomy

    Ⓓ Cambridge

4 Why do you think few people know about the role of William Dawes on that fateful night?

_____

_____

5 Which statement is an opinion?

    Ⓐ Dawes' route was longer than Revere's.

    Ⓑ Revere lied to the British to mislead them.

    Ⓒ Dawes' route was more dangerous than Revere's.

    Ⓓ Dawes and Revere did not make it to Concord that night.

Writing: **Report**

Revolution

★ What interests you about the American Revolution? What happened in families and communities where some people wanted independence, while others were willing to give their allegiance to the king of England? On the Internet and in the library, you can gather information about this topic and hundreds of others related to the Revolution. You might start by accessing the American Revolution at Kid Info:
http://www.kidinfo.com/American_History/American_Revolution.html

With an adult's permission and guidance, gather information from Web sites that are credible, that is, sponsored by a college or university or a historical society. Avoid personal Web sites, as they may contain just one person's opinions.

Then, write a three-page report on some aspect of the American Revolution. After you choose a topic and do some research, you might need to narrow your topic to something you can cover in three pages. The graphic organizer below can help you plan your report. Choose three to five main ideas to cover in your report and then locate details to support each idea. Adjust your outline accordingly.

1. Main idea: _____
    A. Detail: _____
    B. Detail: _____
    C. Detail: _____

2. Main idea: _____
    A. Detail: _____
    B. Detail: _____
    C. Detail: _____

3. Main idea: _____
    A. Detail: _____
    B. Detail: _____
    C. Detail: _____

Name _____

Revolution

⭐ Now write the first draft of your report, using additional paper. Follow the outline you made on page 41. After you explain your main ideas and the details you've gathered, go back and write an introduction that will grab your readers' attention and explain what your report covers. Then, write a conclusion for your report, summarizing what readers can learn from your topic. Finally, think of an interesting title for your report.

_____

_____

_____

_____

_____

_____

_____

_____

_____

_____

_____

_____

_____

After you finish your first draft, look for ways to make it clearer, more complete, and better organized. Ask a friend or family member to read your report and suggest ways to improve it. Together, discuss your ideas and your partner's suggestions.

     Advantage Reading Grade 8 © 2005 Creative Teaching Press

Name _____

Revolution

★ Now write the final draft of your report, using additional paper, if needed. Avoid errors in spelling, punctuation, grammar, and word usage. You might illustrate your report with a photocopy of a picture from a library source, or you might print a photograph or drawing from a Web site.

_____

_____

_____

_____

_____

_____

_____

_____

_____

_____

_____

_____

_____

_____

_____

Your Community's History

Do you live—or did you used to live—in a state that was a colony at the time of the Revolutionary War? Find out what role people from your state played in the war. Learn more about a certain local monument, statue, historical building, or other reminder of your state's participation in the nation's fight for freedom from Great Britain.

Getting a Handle on History

Work with a small group to create a timeline that shows events leading up to the Revolutionary War. You might start by visiting a Web site titled "American During the Age of Revolution" (*http://lcweb2.loc.gov/ammem/bdsds/timeline.html*). Try to include changes and events in a range of categories, such as social, economic, and governmental. You might add illustrations and display your timeline in a school hallway so other students will learn more about our nation's history.

Ride for Freedom

Practice reading aloud the famous poem by Henry Wadsworth Longfellow, "Paul Revere's Ride." Read the stanzas and use your voice to express the emotions in the poem. Make noises like a horse galloping to add to the reading. Then perform the poem for friends and family. Don't forget to provide your audience with some background on this famous ride so they will understand the poem.

Check out these books.

The Revolutionaries by the editors of Time-Life Books
(Time Life-Books)

Revolutionary Citizens: African Americans, 1776–1804 by Daniel C. Littlefield (Oxford University Press)

Sybil's Night Ride by Karen B. Winnick
(Boyds Mills Press)

Victory or Death!: Eight Stories of the American Revolution by Doreen Rappaport and Joan Verniero (HarperCollins)

What's New?

Comprehension: Prior Knowledge

We are bombarded with ads for new gadgets every day. Have you seen the ad for new binoculars that include a digital camera and can record whatever you see? Does that sound like something you would like to buy? Technology is changing rapidly, creating many new products and services to chose from. To explore your knowledge of and attitudes toward new technology, answer questions 1 through 5. There are no right or wrong answers, but this exercise will help you focus on the role—or possible role—of new technology in your life.

1 What is the highest-tech gadget you have ever used? Explain why you consider it to be high tech and whether you thought it was useful.

_____

_____

2 What high-tech gadget would you invent, if you could? Or how would you change an electronic device you use now so it would better meet your needs?

_____

_____

3 What is the most useful high-tech gadget available today? Explain your answer.

_____

_____

4 What percentage of the new gadgets available today do you think we will still be using ten years from now? Explain your answer.

_____

_____

5 What is one gadget that should never have been invented? Explain your choice.

_____

_____

Structural Analysis: Root Words

What's New?

Many English words are based on words from other languages, especially Greek and Latin. These related words share a basic part, called the **root**. If you understand the meaning of root words, you can figure out the meanings of many unfamiliar English words. For example, the Latin root *fig* means "form." Knowing the meaning of this root will help you figure out that the word *effigy* means "an image (form) representing a person."

Study the root definitions below. Then use a word from the box to complete each sentence.

Root	Definition	Root	Definition	Root	Definition	Root	Definition
cert	sure	*grat*	pleasing	*log*	word	*neo*	new
cur	run	*hib*	hold	*lys*	break down	*opt*	best
gam	marriage	*laps*	slip	*minist*	serve	*plur*	more

optimal	administer	neophyte
analysis	inhibit	plurality
excursion	eulogy	monogamy

1 Someone who has just begun to do something is a _____.

2 At a funeral, a friend or family member who talks about the person who died is giving a _____.

3 When you go on an _____, you take a trip.

4 The _____ time for viewing the fall leaves in New England is early October.

5 The nurse started to _____ medicine to the patients.

6 The law was designed to _____ theft.

7 Study the essay and give me your _____ of it.

8 She won because she received a _____ of the votes.

9 In some nations, men are allowed to have several wives, but in the United States only _____ is legal.

Vocabulary: Multiple Meaning Words

⭐ A number of words have more than one meaning, even though the spelling does not change. You can usually determine which meaning is intended in a certain sentence by reading the rest of the sentence or the rest of the paragraph. For example, if you read that soldiers returned to their compound, you know that *compound* means "a walled-in area of buildings," not "a sentence with two clauses" or "a word made from two smaller words." The word *soldiers* is the clue to the correct meaning of *compound* in this sentence.

What's New?

Look for the underlined word in each sentence and choose its correct meaning.

1 The banker returned the money to the vault.
- Ⓐ burial chamber
- Ⓑ leap over a barrier
- Ⓒ room where valuables are kept
- Ⓓ underground storage compartment

2 The tailor will press the seam before finishing the jacket.
- Ⓕ squeeze out juice
- Ⓖ force your way
- Ⓗ make smooth
- Ⓙ reporters

3 The spring was being polluted by fertilizer run-off.
- Ⓐ water coming from the ground
- Ⓑ to jump up suddenly
- Ⓒ March to mid-June
- Ⓓ a coiled wire

4 Don't try that sport unless you are *fit*.
- Ⓕ the right size and shape
- Ⓖ physically healthy
- Ⓗ suitable
- Ⓙ ready

5 Mark the page in your textbook.
- Ⓐ to set apart
- Ⓑ a starting line
- Ⓒ to make a line
- Ⓓ to write a note

6 Did you see the notice about the new class?
- Ⓕ to pay attention to
- Ⓖ to comment on
- Ⓗ announcement
- Ⓙ warning

7 She told me a story about why she was late.
- Ⓐ floor in a building
- Ⓑ fictional narrative
- Ⓒ gossip
- Ⓓ lie

8 When is the employees' morning break?
- Ⓕ to separate into parts
- Ⓖ to make inoperable
- Ⓗ interruption
- Ⓙ to violate

What's New?

Fluency: **Reading with Expression**

⭐ Radio advertisements must interest listeners immediately and convince them to make a purchase—just with the use of voice, music, and sound effects. Read the ad below aloud at least three times, experimenting with changes in your rate and volume to show your excitement about this high-tech cell phone. Then read the ad to friends or family members. If possible, record your ad and play it for them. Afterward, ask if they are convinced to get one of these cell phones.

Impress Your Friends with the Best and Newest Cell Phone!

Would you like to send your friends pictures of what's happening in your life, just like you see in TV commercials? You can! A TopChoice Cell Phone will put cutting-edge technology at your fingertips—and you won't need a degree in computer science to use it! What's more, your camera is actually (this is no joke!) free! You don't buy it. We just send it to you at no cost!

Your new cell phone will have more features than you could dream up! They include a built-in camera with 5 megabytes of memory, along with voice dialing so you don't have to remember any phone numbers—or even push a button. You'll also get voice memo, Internet access, 2-way text messaging, and so much more! You can list up to 500 of your closest friends on the address book—and 300 E-mail and Web addresses. You can set your phone to ring or vibrate, when you just don't want to be interrupted.

All these features sound expensive, right? Remember, I said this phone was free? It really and truly is! The regular price is $230, which is a bargain. But if you start enjoying your new phone by the end of the month, you will get an instant discount of $130! Do the math, and your phone still costs $100, right? Wrong! We will send you a mail-in rebate for that $100. Now your phone is F-R-E-E!

You can choose from a range of calling plans, all designed to meet your needs. Sign up for our family plan, and we'll throw in free long distance! You can call your grandma in California every single day—for nothing!

To order by phone, call 1-958-789-5555. To get the instant rebate, mention our bonus code: 19904. Your friends are waiting to hear from you! So is your grandma!

Name _____

What's New?

Comprehension: Make Inferences

To make an inference, you first consider what you know and what you have read. Next, you draw a conclusion by forming an opinion about the topic. Then you go one step further and apply your conclusion to a broader topic or to another situation. Last, you check your inference to make sure you did not go too far and assume something that does not make sense.

After reading the ad for cell phones on page 48, read each group of statements below and select the option that is a reasonable inference. Notice that some of the options are facts from the ad on page 48, not inferences. Other options are incorrect, based on the ad.

1 Choose the statement that makes a reasonable inference.

    Ⓐ With this cell phone, you can call for free.

    Ⓑ All the calling plans include free long distance.

    Ⓒ Profits from the calling plans pay for the phones.

    Ⓓ Your friends do not need camera phones to receive your pictures.

2 Choose the statement that makes a reasonable inference.

    Ⓕ This phone has the most advanced technology of any on the market.

    Ⓖ This is the only cell phone with these features.

    Ⓗ You will use these features every day.

    Ⓙ This phone will soon be outdated.

3 Choose the statement that makes a reasonable inference.

    Ⓐ This company's calling plans are bargains.

    Ⓑ This company is in business to serve its customers.

    Ⓒ This company has been in business for a long time.

    Ⓓ This company makes a profit from its calling plans.

4 Choose the statement that makes a reasonable inference.

    Ⓕ Having this cell phone will make you very popular.

    Ⓖ Buying a different phone will make you less popular.

    Ⓗ Your grandparents would be pleased if you called more often.

    Ⓙ Cell phones are the best way to keep in touch with friends and family.

Comprehension: Homophones

What's New?

⭐ **Homophones** are words that sound the same but have different meanings and different spellings. One example is the words *their*, *there*, and *they're*. These pairs or groups of words are easily misused. You need to recognize the variations in spelling and understand what each one means.

After reviewing the ad on page 48, read the sentences below, study the words in parentheses, and underline the correct spelling for each sentence.

1 Cell phones are definitely not a fad or (faze/phase).

2 You can enter the phone numbers of (you're/your) friends in the address book.

3 Some plans are so cheap that you can use your phone freely, without (guilt/gilt).

4 Before you (disburse/disperse) your hard-earned money, study the calling plans.

5 Get a plan that (compliments/complements) your lifestyle.

6 You can decide (weather/whether) to set your phone on ring or vibrate.

7 You will certainly impress your (peers/piers) with the camera feature.

8 You (maybe/may be) hesitant to switch phone companies.

9 Some phone companies do (pray/prey) on unsuspecting customers.

10 Their ads contain a (colonel/kernel) of truth.

11 They (pedal/peddle) yesterday's technology at low prices.

12 (Their/There/They're) techniques leave a lot to be desired.

13 The way they mislead potential customers is (vial/vile).

14 The (principal/principle) reason to buy from this company is its long history.

15 Its brochures give you (strait/straight) answers to your questions.

Advantage Reading Grade 8 © 2005 Creative Teaching Press

Vocabulary: Frequently Misspelled Words

What's New?

⭐ Some words are definitely harder to spell than others. Try your hand at spelling the words below. Read each sentence, study the two words in parentheses, and then underline the correct spelling of the word.

1 The waiter pushed two tables together to (accommodate/accomodate) us.

2 I soon received an (acknowledgement/acknowledgment) of my order.

3 The musician was an (amatuer/amateur), but she played well.

4 I will need some (assistance/assistence) with my part in the play.

5 That (cemetary/cemetery) dates back to the Civil War.

6 We must be (conscientious/consciensious) about our use of technology.

7 Are you (eligible/elegible) to receive the discount?

8 Old cell phones are hard to recycle and can harm the (enviroment/environment).

9 Do not (excede/exceed) the number of minutes on your calling plan.

10 Many ads (exagerate/exaggerate) the claims they make for their products.

11 The ad for this new pager makes (extrordinary/extraordinary) claims.

12 Cost can be a (hindrance/hinderance) in taking advantage of technology.

13 The amount of memory in a cell phone is (irrelevant/irrelavent) to me.

14 I would have (prefered/preferred) a less expensive model.

15 Students no longer have the (priviledge/privilege) of carrying a cell phone.

Vocabulary: Content Words

What's New?

Here is an opportunity to test your vocabulary relating to technology, especially to computers. Choose the correct answer for questions 1 through 8. If you aren't sure of an answer, look it up on the Internet or in a recently published encyclopedia.

1 Which term means "to format a disk so it will hold information"?

- Ⓐ scan
- Ⓑ login
- Ⓒ retrieve
- Ⓓ initialize

2 What is a coded instruction used to create Web pages?

- Ⓕ WWW
- Ⓖ HTML
- Ⓗ URL
- Ⓙ FTP

3 Which term means 1,000 bytes?

- Ⓐ megabyte
- Ⓑ gigabyte
- Ⓒ kilobyte
- Ⓓ bit

4 Which term is a tiny piece of silicon with electronic circuits?

- Ⓕ bit
- Ⓖ chip
- Ⓗ byte
- Ⓙ pixel

5 Which term refers to temporary memory?

- Ⓐ ROM
- Ⓑ RAM
- Ⓒ URL
- Ⓓ CPU

6 Which of these is NOT a peripheral?

- Ⓕ keyboard
- Ⓖ monitor
- Ⓗ browser
- Ⓙ mouse

7 What is the smallest part of every image on a monitor?

- Ⓐ bit
- Ⓑ byte
- Ⓒ chip
- Ⓓ pixel

8 What is an extra copy of a file or document?

- Ⓕ software
- Ⓖ network
- Ⓗ backup
- Ⓙ icon

Space Spinoffs

Some Americans think we are spending too much money on our space program. After all, with budgets tight everywhere, can't that money be put to better use right here on Earth? In fact, we all benefit every day from spinoffs from space technology. The products described below are a few of the thousands that help improve our health, strengthen national security, increase productivity—and explore space.

Virtual Reality

Virtual reality began as a NASA project in the mid-1980s. This process combines three-dimensional graphics and sound to create realistic simulations. Equipment built into a helmet or headset allows operators to "step into a scene" and interact with it. Each eye has its own television screen, which makes the image three-dimensional. Sensors in the helmet shift the image as the operators turn their heads. Slightly different sounds coming into each headphone add to the three-dimensional effect. Operators wearing special gloves can "pick up" objects in the scene projected on the TV screens. Tiny vibrators in the gloves allow operators to "feel" what they are picking up.

NASA uses virtual reality to train pilots and astronauts. This tool also helps design engineers understand how fuel flows through a rocket engine, for example. Many other fields use—or will soon use—virtual reality. For instance, architects will be able to walk through a "virtual building." Then they can inspect it for flaws before it is built. Medical students will be able to "operate" on patients. People will be able to "travel" far back in time, perhaps getting to know a tyrannosaurus, up close and personal.

And, as you probably know, virtual reality creates some awesome games!

Protecting the Alaska Pipeline

The Alaska pipeline is 4 feet wide and 800 miles long. It crosses three mountain ranges and many rivers and streams. As the ground under the pipeline freezes and thaws, it rises and drops. These movements weaken the pipeline, risking ruptures and oil spills.

Engineers have solved this problem. They have modified NASA technology used to cool electronic equipment on spacecraft. The supports holding the pipeline now keep the ground underneath permanently frozen, thus reducing the swelling and settling. This technology helps to ensure the safe transport of valuable oil.

Air and Water Purification Systems

NASA's efforts to find ways to provide clean air and water on spacecraft and space stations has paid off on Earth. For at least 20 years, NASA scientists have experimented with natural biological processes that can purify the air and water. One of their first systems used water hyacinths. This floating plant uses sewage for food, absorbing enormous amounts of pollutants from water. The water hyacinth can also be used for fuel and fertilizer and added to cattle feed. Now several towns in the United States use water hyacinths to treat their wastewater.

NASA also developed an artificial marsh to filter pollutants out of water. Sewage-digesting microbes live in a rock bed, along with pollutant-absorbing plants such as bulrushes, reeds, and canna lilies. Now a number of communities use this method to clean their water.

To clean the air, NASA has used plants such as the common philodendron, spider plants, and Chinese evergreens. Engineers created a system that pumps air through a layer of charcoal and through the plants' roots. The pollutants are trapped and digested before the clean air is piped back into the building. Now several companies are selling this system to help clean stale indoor air.

Ski Boots

Back in the 1970s, NASA began developing protective clothing for astronauts, especially those who would visit the moon. Now some of this technology has been modified to produce, among other products, superior ski boots. These high-tech boots have wiring inside that keeps the wearer's feet at just the right temperature. They are also built to be flexible without losing their shape. Some of them are lined with hollow "breathing" pillows. When you slip on the boots, the pillows adapt to your feet. When you buckle the boots, the pillows stop adjusting and hold the shape of your feet.

Other space spinoffs range from enriched baby food to ribbed swimsuits to improve the swimmer's speed in the water. Products to improve health include infrared thermometers that can take your temperature in two seconds and a chip that can diagnosis cancer with no need for surgery. The list also includes improved air tanks for firefighters and life rafts that cannot tip over. If people realized how many spinoffs make their lives easier and healthier, they might want NASA to have a bigger budget!

Reading: Comprehension

After reading the report on pages 53 and 54, answer questions 1 through 5.

1 What is the main idea in this report?

    Ⓐ Technology from the space program created virtual reality.

    Ⓑ We have benefited from the space program in many ways.

    Ⓒ We should increase the budget for the space program.

    Ⓓ The space program has created many spinoffs.

2 Which statement from the report is an opinion?

    Ⓕ Virtual reality has many applications.

    Ⓖ The space program is well worth its cost.

    Ⓗ Space technology has created thousands of spinoffs.

    Ⓙ Keeping the ground frozen under the Alaska pipeline reduces accidents.

3 Why is virtual reality an important tool for astronauts?

    Ⓐ They can pick up objects that are not really there.

    Ⓑ They can practice dangerous tasks without risk.

    Ⓒ They can see a scene in three dimensions.

    Ⓓ They can hear sound in three dimensions.

4 Summarize this report in two or three sentences.

_____

_____

5 Describe an important result of the discovery of the water hyacinth's use in water treatment.

_____

_____

_____

Know the Skill

Cause and Effect
Identifying cause-and-effect relationships helps you understand what you read and hear. A **cause** is an action or problem that results in a change of some kind. An **effect** is a change caused by an action or problem. Often an effect then becomes a cause of another effect, forming a chain of linked causes and effects.

Contemporary fiction is a realistic story and set in the present time. After you read *Wired!*, answer the questions on pages 58 and 59.

Wired!

"Susan, you can't be serious!" Jill rolled her eyes. "I mean, those two guys are definitely geeks! Being seen with them is social suicide!"

Susan sighed. She was afraid Jill would say that, but Alex and Jacob were having so much fun building their robot for the robotics competition that she wanted to be on their team. Besides, judging from the bits of conversation that she had overheard, the robot had some kind of problem, and the boys didn't know how to fix it. Based on what she had heard, she bet it had something to do with the way they had soldered the wires from the switch connecting the motor to the robot's legs. All the time she spent helping her dad in his workshop had taught her a thing or two about motors, for sure, but Jill didn't know that, of course. The most Jill knew about mechanical things was how to insert a CD into her player.

Still, Jill did know one thing: helping the guys with their robot would earn her a new nickname, one she would rather avoid. Now she wished she had never mentioned robots to Jill.

Nevertheless, Susan couldn't help it if Alex and Jacob rode the same bus home from school as she did, and it was just by chance that she ended up sitting behind them while they tried to figure out why their robot wouldn't work right. And how could she know that they would have the robot with them that day?

"I give up!" Alex said as he glared at the robot in his hands. It was made from batteries and lots of wires and had legs that were now wriggling in the air. "The legs move *before* you throw the switch and stop *after* you throw the switch! Old Robbie here is a lunatic, that's all!"

"The competition is only eight days away," Jacob muttered. "We're toast."

"Ummm, how did you guys solder the wires from the switch?" Susan whispered over their shoulders. Fortunately, Jill didn't ride this bus, but several other eighth graders did. Susan hoped they were too busy gabbing with each other to notice her talking to Alex and Jacob.

Advantage Reading Grade 8 © 2005 Creative Teaching Press

Alex turned around in his seat and gave her a fishy look. "What did you say?"

Susan made her mouth smile. "Uh, I was wondering if you connected the NO wire or the NC wire to the motor."

The boys squinted at her as if she had just landed from Mars.

Susan took the squirming robot from Alex and pointed out the wire connected to the motor. "Here's the problem! This is the NC wire. That means the circuit is Normally Closed, or connected. The power is on until you throw the switch, and then the power goes off." She pulled a loose wire out of the robot. "This is the NO wire, which means Normally Open. If you connect this wire instead, Robbie will walk only after you throw the switch." She handed the robot back to Alex, who was staring at her with his mouth open.

"Are you sure? How do you know?" the boys sputtered at the same time.

Susan grinned. "Change the wires and see what happens." She got off the bus after the boys and hadn't been home ten minutes when the phone rang.

"Uh," Jacob mumbled, "your idea worked, kind of, and we—Alex and me—were wondering if you might, umm, come over and see if there's anything else…"

After dinner, Susan walked the two blocks to Jacob's house, her first trip of many. She went over there nearly every night for the next two weeks, helping the boys improve Robbie. When Jill found out about the trips, she was sure Susan had lost her mind.

Finally, it was time for the competition, held in the gym of a nearby high school. Each team had three minutes to demonstrate its robot to the judges. A more complicated robot won first prize, but Robbie came in ninth.

That evening, Susan went to her dad's workshop and started to look for parts she could use for her own robot, which was going to be even more awesome than the one that had won first prize. After all, the next robotics competition was only two months away. Still, maybe she would ask Alex and Jacob to be on her team because they did have some good ideas. Working together from the beginning, they were sure to win first prize.

Searching through piles of spare parts in the workshop, Susan completely forgot to worry about what Jill might think.

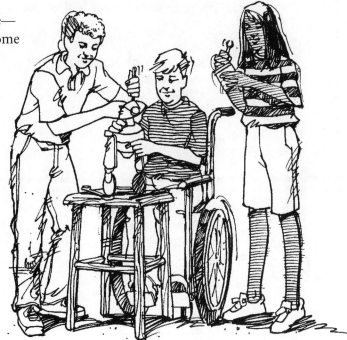

Reading: **Comprehension**

After reading *Wired!* on pages 56 and 57, answer questions 1 through 9.

1 Why does Susan hesitate to help Alex and Jacob with their robot?

- Ⓐ She wants to spend time with Jill.
- Ⓑ She isn't sure what's wrong with it.
- Ⓒ She is worried about what others will think.
- Ⓓ She wants to build her own robot and win the competition.

2 What nickname does Susan not want to be called?

_____

3 What does Jacob mean when he says, "We're toast"?

- Ⓐ We're burnt.
- Ⓑ We've failed.
- Ⓒ We're caught.
- Ⓓ We've got this backwards.

4 What does Jill mean when she says that being seen with the boys is "social suicide"?

- Ⓕ Being seen with them will kill Susan.
- Ⓖ Being seen with Susan will kill the boys.
- Ⓗ Susan will not be popular if she is seen with the boys.
- Ⓙ The boys will not be popular if they are seen with Susan.

Metaphor vs. Slang

A **metaphor** is a comparison of two unlike things without using the words *like* or *as*. For example, if you say, "My calculator became a crutch," you do not mean the calculator helped you walk after you hurt your leg. You mean you relied on the calculator, perhaps too much. The phrase *social suicide* in item 4 is a metaphor. However, the phrase *we're toast* in item 3 is **slang**— informal language.

   Advantage Reading Grade 8 © 2005 Creative Teaching Press

Reading: Comprehension

5 Jill is to *cautious* as Susan is to _____.

    Ⓐ robots

    Ⓑ fearful

    Ⓒ content

    Ⓓ adventurous

6 Do you think Susan and Jill will continue to be friends? Why or why not?

_____

_____

_____

7 Which saying applies to this story?

    Ⓐ An apple a day keeps the doctor away.

    Ⓑ A penny saved is a penny earned.

    Ⓒ Don't judge a book by its cover.

    Ⓓ The early bird gets the worm.

8 Why are Alex and Jacob surprised when Susan offers a suggestion to fix their robot?

    Ⓕ They think she is a geek.

    Ⓖ They don't know who she is.

    Ⓗ They know her suggestion will work.

    Ⓙ They did not expect her to know about mechanical things.

9 What do you think would have happened if changing the wires did not make the robot work? Explain your answer.

_____

_____

_____

Name _____

What's New?

⭐ A spreadsheet looks like a grid. You can use a spreadsheet to work with data or just display it. A spreadsheet is divided into rows labeled with numbers and columns labeled with letters. Each square in this grid is called a cell and has a name. A1 is in the top left corner. Next to it is B1, and under it is A2. In each cell, you can enter words, numbers, symbols, directions, and formulas. The cell you are working in, the active cell, is marked with a dark border.

A spreadsheet works like a calculator because it allows you to add, subtract, multiply, and divide numbers. The "autosum" function will instantly add a whole column or a whole row of numbers. You can use the "sort" function to put numbers in order from low to high—or high to low.

How does a spreadsheet do math? To add two numbers, for example, you first enter the equals sign (=) in a cell. That sign signals that you are going to perform a calculation. Then you enter one number (or the name of its cell on the spreadsheet), the plus sign (+), and the second number (or the name of its cell). After you press enter, the spreadsheet will show you the sum. Of course, you can enter much more complex problems, including algebra formulas.

Study the spreadsheet below and answer the questions on page 61.

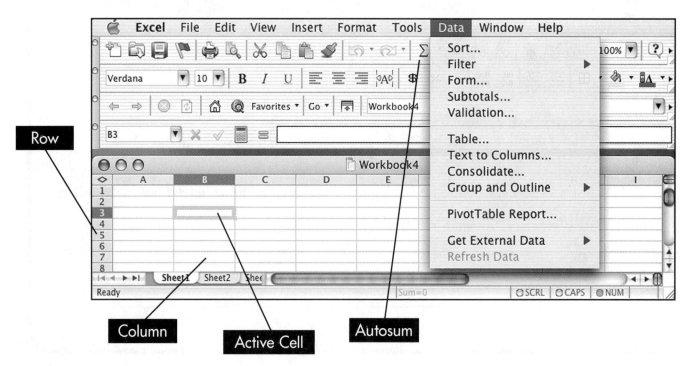

Row

Column

Active Cell

Autosum

Reading: Comprehension

After studying the spreadsheet on page 60, answer questions 1 through 5.

1 You want to put a column of words in alphabetical from the lowest to the highest. Which function will you use?

Ⓐ create chart

Ⓑ equal sign

Ⓒ autosum

Ⓓ sort

2 What is the name of the sixth cell in row C?

_____

3 Look at the toolbars at the top of the spreadsheet. Which function below is not available on this spreadsheet?

Ⓐ using spellcheck

Ⓑ printing the page

Ⓒ cutting text

Ⓓ adding boldface or italics

4 How would you subtract two numbers using the spreadsheet?

_____

_____

_____

5 Which task can you NOT do with a spreadsheet?

Ⓐ draw pictures

Ⓑ make a line graph

Ⓒ compare the prices of two products

Ⓓ figure out each person's share of a group purchase

What's New?

Writing: Multi-Step Directions

⭐ Working with computers and other technology often requires following multi-step directions. Knowing how to write these directions is a valuable skill. Here's an opportunity to strengthen your ability to write directions.

First, think of a process you know how to do that involves at least four steps. For example, can you make a craft, paint a room, install a program on your computer, program a VCR, burn a CD, apply for a part-time job, or perform another process?

After you choose a process to explain, identify and number the main steps. Then, think of the actions that go into each main step and list those as substeps. The outline below will help.

Step 1 _____

    Substep: _____

    Substep: _____

    Substep: _____

Step 2 _____

    Substep: _____

    Substep: _____

    Substep: _____

Step 3 _____

    Substep: _____

    Substep: _____

    Substep: _____

Step 4 _____

    Substep: _____

    Substep: _____

    Substep: _____

What's New?

Writing: Multi-Step Directions

⭐ Now write the first draft of your directions, using additional paper if needed. Following the outline you made on page 62. Begin each step with an active verb, such as *click*, *place*, or *fill*. Number your steps and make sure to list them in chronological order. After each step, you might explain what is supposed to happen, such as "A menu will appear."

After you explain the steps, write an introduction that will prepare readers to carry out the steps. Explain when, why, and who should perform the process. List any needed expertise, supplies, or equipment. Finally, think of an informative title for your directions.

_____

_____

_____

_____

_____

_____

_____

_____

_____

_____

_____

After you finish your first draft, look for ways to make it clearer, more complete, and better organized. Ask a friend or family member to read your directions and try to follow them. Then discuss any confusion that arose and how you might clarify your directions.

What's New?

Writing: **Multi-Step Directions**

⭐ Now write the final draft of your directions, using additional paper if necessary. Avoid errors in spelling, punctuation, grammar, and word usage. You might illustrate your directions with one or more diagrams.

_____

_____

_____

_____

_____

_____

_____

_____

_____

_____

_____

_____

_____

_____

_____

_____

_____

Learn More about Space Spinoffs

To read more about the thousands of space spinoffs, you might start with this Web site: *www.sti.nasa.gov/tto/spinoff.html*. It provides many NASA-related sites, along with links to a NASA publication titled *Spinoff*. Another excellent site is *www.thespaceplace.com/nasa/spinoffs.html*. Your class might select interesting spinoffs and describe one each day as part of your school's morning announcements.

Fun with Robotics

Does your school or community have a group that builds robots? Many young people enjoy the challenge of building robots from junk, for fun or for a competition. To learn more, you might visit this Web site: *www.usfirst.org*. *FIRST* stands for "For Inspiration and Recognition of Science and Technology." More than 7,000 students competed in its first robotics championship.

Use a Spreadsheet

Practice using a spreadsheet. For example, you might record your progress in a sport. Put the days down the left side of the spreadsheet and your running or swimming times, for example, in the first column. You might include additional columns for the number of push-ups you did that day, for instance.

Or you could record your earnings for each week, along with any costs involved, such as the cost of gas if you mow lawns. If you deliver papers, you could use a spreadsheet to keep track of which customers have paid. See how spreadsheets can help you organize your life.

Check out these books.

Absolute Beginner's Guide to Building Robots by Gareth Branwyn (Que)
Robot Building for Dummies by Roger Arrick and Nancy Stevenson (For Dummies)

Good Sport, Good Health

Comprehension: Prior Knowledge

What do you know about the relationship between sports and health? Using what you already know, write a paragraph or two that answers as many of the questions below as possible, in any order.

- What are some ways that sports in general can improve your physical health? Your emotional health? Your social health and relationships with others?
- Which specific sports do you think are best at strengthening a person's physical health? Emotional health? Social health? Which sports, if any, do you think can improve someone's intelligence and thinking?
- Why do many people enjoy playing sports? Why do they enjoy watching sports?
- Why do many people avoid playing or even trying a sport?

_____

_____

_____

_____

_____

_____

_____

_____

_____

_____

_____

_____

Advantage Reading Grade 8 © 2005 Creative Teaching Press

Structural Analysis: **Affixes**

Good Sport, Good Health

⭐ An **affix** is a group of words that is added to the beginning (prefix) or the end (suffix) of a word. Affixes can change the meaning of a word and/or its part of speech. Knowing the meanings of affixes can help you determine the meanings of unfamiliar words.

Prefix	Definition	Suffix	Definition
contra-	against	*-archy*	government
counter-	opposite	*-ate*	to make
eu-	good	*-ent*	inclined to
extra-	outside	*-ism*	a practice or process
hept-	seven	*-ous*	outside
mal-	bad		
per-	through		
peri-	around		

Look at the lists of prefixes and suffixes Use this information to choose words from the box to answer questions 1 through 8. Some words may be new to you, but the affixes will help you choose correctly.

pericardium	malevolent	permeates	contraband
euphemism	heptarchy	extraneous	countermand

1 When a smell spreads across a room, it _____ the room.

2 Illegal goods are also called _____.

3 A vicious person might be described as _____.

4 A positive expression used in place of a negative one is a _____.

5 A combination of seven British kingdoms in the seventh and eighth centuries was called a _____.

6 The lining surrounding the heart is the _____.

7 Information that is not needed is _____.

8 A direction to stop _____ a direction to go.

Vocabulary: **Analogies**

Good Sport, Good Health

Analogies test your understanding of the relationships between pairs of words. An analogy consists of a pair of words, followed by a single word. For example:

Book is to student as hammer is to _____ .

A student uses a book, so the analogy should be completed with a word that tells who uses a hammer—a carpenter. Analogies might also involve other relationships, such as synonyms or antonyms, cause-effect, sequence, part-whole, object-action, and object-use.

Study the analogies below. Figure out how the first pair of words is related, and then choose the correct word to complete the second pair.

1. *Swimmer* is to *goggles* as *doctor* is to _____.
   - Ⓐ stethoscope
   - Ⓑ hospital
   - Ⓒ patient
   - Ⓓ nurse

2. *Book* is to *character* as *salad* is to _____.
   - Ⓕ carrots
   - Ⓖ dinner
   - Ⓗ desert
   - Ⓙ plot

3. *Six* is to *three* as *twelve* is to _____.
   - Ⓐ three
   - Ⓑ four
   - Ⓒ six
   - Ⓓ nine

4. *Volcano* is to *destruction* as *fertilizer* is to _____.
   - Ⓕ plants
   - Ⓖ growth
   - Ⓗ farmers
   - Ⓙ insecticide

5. *Bird* is to *flock* as *fish* is to _____.
   - Ⓐ carp
   - Ⓑ water
   - Ⓒ ocean
   - Ⓓ school

6. *Strawberry* is to *fruit* as *skirt* is to _____.
   - Ⓕ vegetables
   - Ⓖ clothing
   - Ⓗ uniform
   - Ⓙ pants

7. *Star* is to *constellation* as *hand* is to _____.
   - Ⓐ telescope
   - Ⓑ finger
   - Ⓒ clock
   - Ⓓ foot

8. *Piano* is to *music* as *automobile* is to _____.
   - Ⓕ walking
   - Ⓖ repairs
   - Ⓗ travel
   - Ⓙ bus

 Advantage Reading Grade 8 © 2005 Creative Teaching Press

Good Sport, Good Health

Fluency: **Reading with Expression**

⭐ Read this readers' theater script aloud, using your voice to add meaning and interest to the performance. There are two parts in this script. Use a different voice for each part. After practicing at least three times, perform this readers' theater for one or more friends or family members. Be sure to pronounce the words clearly so they will understand you easily.

To Try or Not to Try

Bonnie   I've heard that before! The next thing you know, the coach is giving the old speech about how tough it was to decide who would be on the team. And then the list of the ones who made it gets posted on the bulletin board, but somehow they keep forgetting to put my name on it. Anyway, if I were meant to be on the swim team, I'd have gills, but here I am, still gill-less, so I guess I'll just have to excel at another sport. How about boxing? I bet I'd be a star on the school boxing team.

Alice   Not even if our school had a boxing team. Bonnie, I've seen you swim a hundred times! I'm sure that's the sport you're cut out for. As a matter of fact, I kind of told the coach you were going to try out, so you can't back down now.

Bonnie   Back down? You're getting on my nerves! I can't back down because I never said I'd do it in the first place. You've just got to break down and tell the coach you made a mistake 'cause I'm not going to try out.

Alice   Well, Grandma Henry will sure be disappointed to hear that.

Bonnie   Come again? You told your grandmother I was going to try out? How could you do that to me, Alice?

Alice   Well, you know how much she likes you. I knew she'd be happy if I told her you were trying out for the swim team with me. She was, too. But you can put an end to her happiness right away and tell her you chickened out.

Bonnie   Ugh! Why do I put up with you? Bring on the try-outs!

Good Sport, Good Health

Comprehension: **Predict Outcomes**

As you read, you might predict what will happen next or what a certain character might do next. You are combining what you have read so far with your own experiences in similar situations. As you read, you must check your predictions against the new information you are gaining. If the new information does not support your predictions, you must change them.

After reading *To Try or Not to Try* on page 69, answer questions 1 through 4.

1 As this readers' theater begins, you might predict that Bonnie will not try out for the swim team. Which detail supports this prediction?

 Ⓐ Bonnie has tried out for teams before and not been chosen.

 Ⓑ Bonnie wants to be on the school's boxing team.

 Ⓒ Alice points out that Bonnie is a strong swimmer.

 Ⓓ Alice says Bonnie just has to do her best.

2 What prediction would you make about the future of the friendship between Alice and Bonnie? Give reasons for your answer.

_____

_____

3 As the readers' theater continues, what is the first hint that the prediction that Bonnie will not try out is incorrect?

 Ⓐ Alice tells Bonnie not to back down.

 Ⓑ Alice tells Grandma Henry that Bonnie will try out.

 Ⓒ Bonnie says Alice should tell the coach that she is not trying out.

 Ⓓ Bonnie finds out Grandma Henry thinks she is going to try out.

4 What prediction would you make about the results of Bonnie trying out? Give reasons for your prediction.

_____

_____

Advantage Reading Grade 8 © 2005 Creative Teaching Press

Good Sport, Good Health

Comprehension: Idioms

An **idiom** is a group of words that does not mean exactly what it says. For example, if someone tells you to "Get the show on the road," you know you aren't expected to travel around entertaining people. Instead, you are supposed to get started doing something.

Read each underlined idiom from *To Try or Not to Try* on page 69 and choose the answer that correctly states its meaning.

1 You just have to <u>give it your best</u>.
- Ⓐ perform to your limits
- Ⓑ perform for the crowd
- Ⓒ give away something you really like
- Ⓓ give the best present you've ever given

2 I'm sure that's the sport <u>you're cut out for</u>.
- Ⓕ you're meant to do
- Ⓖ you will try out for
- Ⓗ you cut out of your life
- Ⓙ you will get hurt doing

3 You can't <u>back down</u> now!
- Ⓐ turn around
- Ⓑ go backwards
- Ⓒ go downstairs
- Ⓓ change your mind

4 You're <u>getting on my nerves</u>!
- Ⓕ stepping on my toes
- Ⓖ getting in my way
- Ⓗ annoying me
- Ⓙ crowding me

5 You've just got to <u>break down</u> and tell him.
- Ⓐ fall down
- Ⓑ make time
- Ⓒ stop avoiding it
- Ⓓ break your promise

6 <u>Come again</u>?
- Ⓕ Will you return?
- Ⓖ Are you coming?
- Ⓗ What did you say?
- Ⓙ Why did you do that?

7 Why do I <u>put up with you</u>?
- Ⓐ try out with you
- Ⓑ reach up with you
- Ⓒ accept what you do
- Ⓓ do what you tell me

8 <u>Bring on</u> the try-outs!
- Ⓕ I'm ready for the try-outs!
- Ⓖ Take me to the try-outs!
- Ⓗ Bring the try-outs here!
- Ⓙ Schedule the try-outs!

Name _____

Good Sport, Good Health

Vocabulary: Frequently Misused Words

Some pairs or groups of words are so similar that the words are often confused and used incorrectly. Some word pairs sound nearly alike but have different meanings, while others are pronounced differently but have meanings that are easily confused. You must be familiar with the meanings of similar words so you can determine which word to use.

Read each sentence and think about the meanings of the words in parentheses. Then underline the correct word for that sentence.

1. We were late for the second (cession/session) of the training program.

2. He tied the box shut with a strong (chord/cord).

3. She spent most of her time with a small (clique/click) of friends.

4. The fantastic sunrise was a (cymbal/symbol) of good things to come.

5. The backpack served a (duel/dual) purpose.

6. Two elderly people (feinted/fainted) in the oppressive heat.

7. Bus (fair/fare) was included in the cost of the trip.

8. She was (fined/find) as a result of her speeding ticket.

9. My brother has a (flair/flare) for painting with watercolors.

10. The storm brought (hale/hail) the size of a dime.

11. Do you need another (hangar/hanger) for those clothes?

12. The homeless man had a (horde/hoard) of food under the floorboard.

13. His presence was enough to (insight/incite) a riot.

14. Did you (ensure/insure) your new car yet?

15. The bank had a (lean/lien) against the house.

     Advantage Reading Grade 8 © 2005 Creative Teaching Press

Vocabulary: Content Words

Good Sport, Good Health

Here is your opportunity to see how many health- and sports-related terms you know. Choose the correct answer for questions 1 through 8. If you aren't sure of an answer, look up the term in an encyclopedia.

1 What kind of exercise continually uses large amounts of oxygen?
- Ⓐ aerobic
- Ⓑ isotonic
- Ⓒ isometric
- Ⓓ anaerobic

2 Which term describes the ability of muscles to keep performing without fatigue?
- Ⓕ flexibility
- Ⓖ endurance
- Ⓗ strength
- Ⓙ agility

3 What is an inflammation of the joints that can make moving painful?
- Ⓐ arthritis
- Ⓑ osteoporosis
- Ⓒ hypothermia
- Ⓓ heat exhaustion

4 What technique will develop additional strength in a muscle?
- Ⓕ warm up
- Ⓖ overload
- Ⓗ stretching
- Ⓙ cool down

5 Which of these is a benefit of flexibility?
- Ⓐ lower blood pressure
- Ⓑ increased endurance
- Ⓒ reduced stroke risk
- Ⓓ fewer injuries

6 Which term relates to the amount of resistance during exercise?
- Ⓕ frequency
- Ⓖ stretching
- Ⓗ flexibility
- Ⓙ intensity

7 Which skill is the ability to change positions rapidly
- Ⓐ reaction time
- Ⓑ coordination
- Ⓒ balance
- Ⓓ agility

8 What does RICE stand for?
- Ⓕ Resuscitation, Infection, Concussion, Emergency
- Ⓖ Rest, Ice, Compression, Elevation
- Ⓗ Remove, Insert, Cover, Ease
- Ⓙ Resist, Inject, Cool, Effect

Is Cross-Training for You?

If you are a distance runner, should your training consist only of running long distances? Or is it also beneficial to do some yoga, lift weights, or swim laps?

Cross-training means performing two or more types of exercise in one workout or doing them in successive workouts. However, not everyone agrees that cross-training is effective. Many athletes and their trainers follow the principle of specificity: exercise should be specific to the athlete's goals. These people believe that lifting weights, for example, is a waste of time for runners because it does not help them run faster. These critics point out that different sports put different demands on athletes. For instance, runners need strong calf muscles, but cyclers must develop huge quadriceps.

On the other hand, the human body is a complex machine. It requires many kinds of exercise to perform at its peak. For instance, runners need aerobic fitness to sprint across the finish line, and swimming helps build this type of fitness. Flexibility helps prevent injuries, so stretching is a valuable addition to any exercise program. Upper-body strength can help prevent fatigue for distance runners. Lifting weights helps to build muscles, which aids most athletes. In fact, studies have shown that weight training helps tennis players increase the speed of their serves and baseball players throw faster pitches. After weight training, basketball players in one study were able to jump higher.

Cross-training also has other benefits, such as adding variety to a training program. Instead of just running for hours, for example, the athlete might also swim, bicycle, work out on machines, or have fun with in-line skating.

Advantage Reading Grade 8 © 2005 Creative Teaching Press

If you are considering cross-training, be aware of some cautions. First, start a new kind of exercise slowly. Save the five-mile cycling trip until after you have developed more strength in your quadriceps. An hour on a new machine is undoubtedly too long. Shorten your first couple of workouts in a new exercise to 20 minutes or less.

If you are a serious athlete with a firm training schedule, don't add cross-training to it. Instead, substitute a new exercise for something you are already doing, at least at first. Also, if you are considering cross-training because of an injury, don't choose a new exercise that will worsen that injury. For example, runners with an injured quadricep should not add cycling to their training program.

Here are some common types of exercise that can become part of your cross training program:

Type of Exercise	Benefits	Examples
Aerobic and anaerobic	Build endurance, flexibility, and strength	Aerobic: power walking, running, swimming, skating, water exercises, cycling, rowing Anaerobic: sprinting in any of the above exercises
Weight training	Increases muscle strength	Hand weights or machines, isometrics
Stretching	Improves flexibility	Yoga

If your exercise program leaves you physically tired, you probably should stop exercising for a day or two and re-evaluate your overall health. However, if exercising leaves you mentally tired, cross-training could help you look forward to working out. If a friend trains in a different sport, you might try training together. You both will benefit, physically and mentally!

Reading: **Comprehension**

After reading the report on pages 74 and 75, answer questions 1 through 5.

1 What is the main idea in this report?

Ⓐ Cross-training is beneficial for runners.

Ⓑ Training should match the sport.

Ⓒ Every athlete should cross train.

Ⓓ Cross-training can be beneficial.

2 What are two reasons why many athletes cross train?

_____

_____

3 How could cross-training be harmful?

Ⓐ It wastes training time.

Ⓑ The athlete might become bored.

Ⓒ It trains muscles the athlete doesn't need.

Ⓓ The athlete might overdo it in a new sport.

4 How could you decide whether to try cross-training?

_____

_____

5 Which generalization is based on this report?

Ⓐ Everyone should cross-train.

Ⓑ Training for a sport will keep you healthy.

Ⓒ Schools should require students to train for a sport.

Ⓓ A broad approach can be more helpful than a narrow one.

Know **Skill** 👉

Make Generalizations
When you make a generalization, you gather information, draw a conclusion, and then apply that conclusion to your life. Next, you must evaluate your generalization to see if it is valid. Does it make sense? Do you need to add a limiting word, such as *some*, *many*, or *usually*?

     Advantage Reading Grade 8 © 2005 Creative Teaching Press

Contemporary fiction refers to stories that are realistic and set in the present time. After you read the story on pages 77 and 78, answer the questions on page 79.

The Test

The team was in the locker room, gearing up for a tough game against the Warriors, their biggest rivals. Maurice and Tyler were standing side by side in front of their lockers, pulling on their pads and uniforms. Shouts, insults, and laughter echoed through the room, signs that tension was higher than usual for this game.

Maurice was adjusting his shoulder pads when he glanced over and noticed that Ty was rubbing something onto his shoulders. "You're using hand cream, Ty?" Maurice shook his head. "That's girl stuff, man! Those pads are going to slip right off your shoulders during the game. Won't that be funny?"

Tyler grinned and handed the tube of cream to Maurice. "It's not hand cream, dummy!" he whispered. "It's The Cream, magic stuff that's going to help me be the best fullback this school has ever seen. In fact, it's going to get me a scholarship to any college I want!"

Maurice frowned as he studied the shiny tube. "There isn't any label. Where did you get this stuff, anyway? It's not something illegal, is it, Ty? If you can't pass the school drug test, you're history on the team, you know, and you sure aren't getting any scholarships."

Tyler shot him a sharp look. "Keep your voice down! Anyway, a drug test won't be any problem for me." He leaned closer and whispered, "This stuff is specially made so it won't show up in a drug test. What's more, you can rub it on any muscle that you want to get bigger! How about that?"

Maurice squinted at his friend. "It's a steroid then?"

Tyler grabbed Maurice's arm and jerked him closer until they were nose to nose. "Be quiet, man! Do you want to get me in trouble?"

Maurice shook his arm free and stepped back. "I think you're already there, Ty."

Ty's face darkened. "No, where I am is in charge of my life. You're a good player, Mo, but you could be great, if you wanted to. Look at my shoulders. Can't you see the power there? I'm getting bigger every week 'cause of this cream. I usually just use it at home, but I figured a little extra before the big game will give me that special edge, you know?"

"I am looking at your shoulders, Ty, and I see all kinds of pimples there. I never noticed them before. It's that cream, isn't it?" asked Maurice.

Tyler shrugged. "So what? No one sees my shoulders, usually." Then he grinned and flexed his muscles. "They just see what I can do on the field with all this power!"

Now Maurice was looking at Tyler's chest. "Uh, Ty, I see a bigger problem than those pimples. You're going to need my little sister's training bra pretty soon."

His face turning purple, Ty dropped the tube and grabbed Maurice's throat with both hands. "That's it!" he said through clenched teeth. "I've had enough from you! You're just jealous that I'm more of a man than you are!"

The locker room was so noisy that only the players standing close by heard the crash as Tyler forced Maurice down on the locker room floor and straddled him, squeezing his neck tighter and tighter. The other players stared at the two friends for a second, but then several of them pulled Ty off Maurice and held him down on the floor.

Maurice sat up, holding his throat and coughing. Ty's fingerprints were outlined in red on his neck.

When Maurice glanced up, Coach Stevenson was standing over them with his arms crossed. "So is this a big problem or just jitters before the game?" Coach asked sternly.

Maurice didn't know what to say. It sure was a big problem, but probably not what the coach had in mind. Just then, Coach Stevenson noticed a shiny tube lying on the floor beside Maurice. He grabbed it, squeezed some cream into his hand, and sniffed it. Watching him, Ty, still sitting on the floor, groaned and turned his head toward the wall.

"Whose is this?" Coach Stevenson asked, his voice just above a whisper.

After several seconds of absolute silence, Ty muttered, "It's mine, just some cream to help with some pimples on my shoulders. They bother me under the pads, you know…." He stopped when he glanced up and saw the coach's expression.

Coach Stevenson turned to the team. "Finish suiting up. It's almost time for the kickoff. Tyler won't be playing today, so Jacob will take his place."

As the other players moved away, a few locker doors banged, but no one said a word. Ty was staring up at the coach, panic in his face. "But I have to play tonight, Coach! That's just cream! I can prove it! Give me a drug test!"

"I've already given you a test, Tyler, and you failed."

Advantage Reading Grade 8 © 2005 Creative Teaching Press

Reading: **Comprehension**

After reading *The Test* on pages 77 and 78, answer questions 1 through 5.

1 Which event is part of the rising action in the story, leading to the climax?

Ⓐ The coach says Ty failed a test.

Ⓑ The team is getting dressed for the game.

Ⓒ Ty doesn't notice that he dropped the tube.

Ⓓ The coach tells Ty he can't play in the game.

2 How do you think Coach Stevenson knew the cream was an illegal drug?

_____

_____

_____

3 Which of these was NOT caused by the steroid cream?

Ⓐ Ty was forbidden from playing in the game.

Ⓑ Ty wanted to be a star football player.

Ⓒ Ty had started to look like a girl.

Ⓓ Ty got angry very quickly.

4 The coach tells Ty that he has already failed a test. What does the coach mean?

_____

_____

5 Which event came first in the story?

Ⓐ Ty says he's not worried about a drug test.

Ⓑ Maurice thinks Ty is using hand cream.

Ⓒ Maurice guesses what is in the tube.

Ⓓ Ty starts using the cream.

Know **the** **Skill**

Sequence
Sequence refers to the order in which steps should be completed or the actions or events that occur in a story or article. Understanding this sequence will help you better understand what you read. Sequence is often related to cause and effect: one event causes the next one, often resulting in a chain of linked events.

Name _____

Good Sport, Good Health

Graphic Information: Bar Graphs

⭐ Do you look forward to physical education class, or would you rather avoid it? Are PE classes providing what most students really want? One study asked 500 middle school students to rate their physical education classes. Study the three bar graphs below with their responses and then answer the questions on page 81.

What Students Like About PE

| The opportunity to exercise | Getting fit | It's fun | The activities offered |
| 20% | 18% | 16% | 16% |

What Students Do Not Like About PE

| Running | Boring activities/no variety | Dressing/undressing for class |
| 13% | 9% | 7% |

What Students Would Like in PE

| Learn how to stay fit | Skills and rules for activities | Learn how the body works |
| 52% | 20% | 10% |

Source: National Association for Sport and Physical Education

Name _____

Reading: Comprehension

After studying the bar graphs on page 80, answer questions 1 through 5.

1 Which conclusion is accurate, based on these graphs?

    Ⓐ Changing clothes in PE is a major concern for young people.

    Ⓑ Students really want to know how their bodies work.

    Ⓒ Students like exercise as long as it isn't running.

    Ⓓ Most students just want to have fun in PE.

2 The numbers in the graphs are percentages. Why aren't they shown in a pie chart or circle graph?

_____

_____

3 Which statement describes the students in this study accurately?

    Ⓐ About 250 want to learn how to stay fit.

    Ⓑ About 20 want the opportunity to exercise.

    Ⓒ About 100 want to learn how their bodies work.

    Ⓓ About 20 want PE to teach them skills and rules.

4 Which of these topics did the students in the study feel most strongly about?

    Ⓕ running

    Ⓖ learning how to stay fit

    Ⓗ the opportunity to exercise

    Ⓙ learning skills and rules for activities

5 How do your own attitudes toward physical education classes compare with the findings in these three bar graphs?

_____

_____

_____

Name _____

Good Sport, Good Health

Writing: **Biography**

★ A biography describes all or part of someone's life and is written by another person. You may have already read several biographies as a school assignment or because you wanted to learn more about a certain person.

Now you will write a biography of another person, living or deceased. For this assignment, choose someone who is related to sports or health in some way. This might be a professional sports player, a coach at your school, or someone who has encouraged you to play a sport or to take care of your health, such as a family member, neighbor, someone at school, or a youth leader.

The graphic organizer below will help you organize this information. You might change the order in which you present this information in your biography or weave two topics together, such as family history and places the person lived.

Person's name (and possibly relationship to writer)
Birth (and death) date
Birthplace and early life
Education
Marriage and family history
Places this person lived
Personality
Accomplishments
Other information

   Advantage Reading Grade 8 © 2005 Creative Teaching Press

Good Sport, Good Health

Writing: **Biography**

⭐ After you have gathered information, write the first draft of your biography, using additional paper if needed. Incorporate information from your organizer on page 82, changing the order of topics, if you wish. Your introduction should interest readers and help explain why you chose to write about this person. End your biography with a conclusion that summarizes this person's accomplishments and contributions and again makes it clear why you wrote about him or her. Don't forget to begin your biography with an interesting title.

_____

_____

_____

_____

_____

_____

_____

_____

_____

_____

_____

After you finish your first draft, look for ways to make it clearer, more complete, and better organized. Ask a partner, friend, or family member to read it and suggest improvements. For example, you might need to add more details about the person's personality.

Name _____

Good Sport, Good Health

Writing: Biography

⭐ Now write the final draft of your biography, using extra sheets of paper if necessary. Consider your partner's editing suggestions and avoid errors in spelling, punctuation, grammar, and word usage. You might illustrate your biography with a photograph of this person.

_____

_____

_____

_____

_____

_____

_____

_____

_____

_____

_____

_____

_____

_____

_____

_____

Advantage Reading Grade 8 © 2005 Creative Teaching Press

Try Out!

With a small group, list activities in your school and community that require participants to try out. Besides sports, possibilities include trying out for a part in a play, a choir, or the school band. Then, perhaps with a partner, sign up and try out for an activity. Even if you are not chosen, the experience of trying out will help you prepare for a time when you really want something, such as a job!

Cross-Train

If you already play a sport, think about ways you could cross-train. For example, if you play basketball, you might try swimming or cycling. Playing more than one sport helps you develop more skills, interact with more people, and have more fun.

Be Heard

Consider what you like or do not like about the physical education program at your school. Then, perhaps with a group of classmates, write a letter to the appropriate person or group, such as the PE teacher, the school principal, or the board of education. Explain what you enjoy and think is valuable about your school's PE program and then politely suggest realistic changes, including strong reasons for your suggestions.

Check out these books.

Be Healthy! It's a Girl Thing: Food Fitness and Feeling Great by Mavis Jukes and Lilian Cheung (Crown)

Careers for Health Nuts & Others Who Like to Stay Fit by Blythe Camenson (VGM Career Books)

Fitness for Health and Sports by Patricia G. Avila (Penmarin Books)

Also look for books about your favorite sport or a sport you would like to know more about. You'll have many choices! In addition, you can find biographies of many sports heroes from Lance Armstrong, to Ken Griffey, Jr., to Mia Hamm.

Name _____

Have Fun!

Comprehension: Prior Knowledge

The phrase *Have fun!* means different things to different people. Do you ever wonder how people decide what's fun and what's not, what's exciting and what's boring, what's hilarious and what's offensive? To explore this topic, answer the questions below. You do not need to share your responses with anyone, if you would rather not.

1 What are some ways that you have fun, alone or with others?

_____

_____

_____

2 Do you enjoy the same kinds of fun as your friends? Why do you think that is so?

_____

_____

_____

3 What are some things that others think are fun, but you do not?

_____

_____

_____

4 What kinds of things seem to be fun for nearly everyone?

_____

_____

_____

5 What kinds of entertainment or activities would you like to enjoy more often?

_____

_____

_____

Comprehension: Similes and Metaphors

Have Fun!

Writers use similes and metaphors as a colorful way to describe people, objects, ideas, and experiences. A **simile** is a comparison of two unlike things using the words *like* or *as*. Here is an example: *He was as content as a child with a cookie.* A **metaphor** also compares two unlike things, but it does not use the words *like* or *as*. This sentence uses a metaphor: *The cookie was a rock in my stomach.*

Choose the sentence that best explains this simile or metaphor.

1 His offer to help was as rare as a white tiger.

- Ⓐ His help was very special, like a white tiger.
- Ⓑ He offered to help save the white tigers.
- Ⓒ He was as rare as a white tiger.
- Ⓓ He did not often offer to help.

2 Her lateness was as certain as thunder after lightning.

- Ⓕ She was always late.
- Ⓖ She was late because of a storm.
- Ⓗ It was lightning when she arrived.
- Ⓙ The thunder came later, after the lightning.

3 He was as annoying as a little brother.

- Ⓐ He wished he didn't have a little brother.
- Ⓑ He was annoyed with his little brother.
- Ⓒ He was acting like a child.
- Ⓓ He was aggravating.

4 He was a carnivore in a rabbit hutch.

- Ⓕ He ate only meat.
- Ⓖ He took advantage of people.
- Ⓗ He was feeding meat to the rabbits.
- Ⓙ The rabbits were afraid of the meat-eater.

5 She was a peacock, preparing to greet her admirers.

- Ⓐ She was birdlike.
- Ⓑ She wore brightly colored clothing.
- Ⓒ She was very concerned about peacocks.
- Ⓓ She was very concerned about her appearance.

Name _____

Have Fun!

⭐ The dictionary definition of a word is its denotative meaning. However, many words also have a connotative meaning: that is, they have emotional associations. Thus, if something smells, you might call it a scent or an odor. While scent and odor have a similar denotative meaning, scent has a positive connotative meaning, while odor has a negative, unpleasant association. As you write, you must be aware of connotative meanings and use the words that express your ideas clearly.

Read each sentence below and review the word choices. Each group of words has a similar denotative meaning, but different connotative meanings. Choose the connotative meaning that best fits the sentence.

1 The _____ politely applauded the speaker's remarks.

   Ⓐ fellowship
   Ⓑ crowd
   Ⓒ gang
   Ⓓ mob

2 They built their dream house on _____ lot.

   Ⓕ a deserted
   Ⓖ an empty
   Ⓗ a barren
   Ⓙ a bleak

3 After the accident, he _____ with difficulty.

   Ⓐ paced
   Ⓑ walked
   Ⓒ strolled
   Ⓓ sauntered

4 The detective _____ the suspect.

   Ⓕ chatted with
   Ⓖ talked with
   Ⓗ spoke with
   Ⓙ questioned

5 The family lived in a run-down _____ near an abandoned warehouse.

   Ⓐ house
   Ⓑ cabin
   Ⓒ shack
   Ⓓ home

6 Joseph had few friends because he was so _____.

   Ⓕ communicative
   Ⓖ conversational
   Ⓗ talkative
   Ⓙ gossipy

Name _____

Have Fun!

⭐ Gene Ziegler wrote the poem below, which is part of a longer poem, after his two young grandsons "significantly rearranged the resources" on his computer. The poem is fun, but not easy to read aloud. Read it aloud at least three times, until you can do it quickly and clearly. Then read the poem to friends or family members. (A *gauss* is a unit used to measure the strength of a magnetic field. *Souse* means "cover something with liquid.")

A Grandchild's Guide to Using Grandpa's Computer

by Gene Ziegler

Here's an easy game to play.
Here's an easy thing to say...

If a packet hits a pocket on a socket on a port,
And the bus is interrupted as a very last resort,
And the address of the memory makes your floppy disk abort,
Then the socket packet pocket has an error to report!

If your cursor finds a menu item followed by a dash,
And the double-clicking icon puts your window in the trash,
And your data is corrupted 'cause the index doesn't hash,
Then your situation's hopeless, and your system's gonna crash!

You can't say this? What a shame, sir!
We'll find you another game, sir.

If the label on the cable on the table at your house,
Says the network is connected to the button on your mouse,
But your packets want to tunnel on another protocol,
That's repeatedly rejected by the printer down the hall,
And your screen is all distorted by the side effects of gauss,
So your icons in the window are as wavy as a souse,
Then you may as well reboot and go out with a bang,
'Cause as sure as I'm a poet, the sucker's gonna hang!

When the copy of your floppy's getting sloppy on the disk,
And the microcode instructions cause unnecessary risk,
Then you have to flash your memory and you'll want to ram your ROM.
Quickly turn off the computer and be sure to tell your mom!

Comprehension: Multiple-Meaning Words

Have Fun!

⭐ Some words have more than one meaning, but the context can usually help you determine which meaning is being used. For instance, a tire could be the rubber around a wheel, or it could mean "to become weary." If your uncle says he has a flat tire, though, you know he's not telling you he's worn out.

Read each line below, taken from the poem on page 89, and think about the meaning of the underlined word and the context. Then select its meaning in that sentence.

1 If a packet hits a pocket on a socket on a <u>port</u>,
  Ⓐ a place where two devices connect
  Ⓑ the left side of a ship or airplane
  Ⓒ a place where ships dock
  Ⓓ a window in a ship

2 And the <u>bus</u> is interrupted
  Ⓕ a vehicle that carries passengers
  Ⓖ a transmission path
  Ⓗ to clear a table
  Ⓙ a kiss

3 as a very last <u>resort</u>,
  Ⓐ to go somewhere frequently
  Ⓑ a place to vacation
  Ⓒ to sort again
  Ⓓ possibility

4 If your cursor finds a menu item followed by a <u>dash</u>,
  Ⓕ a short run
  Ⓖ a punctuation mark
  Ⓗ a pinch of something
  Ⓙ to knock or hurl something

5 And your data is corrupted 'cause the index doesn't <u>hash</u>,
  Ⓐ a dish made with chopped food
  Ⓑ to restate something
  Ⓒ to talk things over
  Ⓓ a computer term

6 And your <u>screen</u> is all distorted by the side effects of gauss,
  Ⓕ to separate into parts
  Ⓖ to view a motion picture
  Ⓗ something that shields and protects
  Ⓙ the surface where an image appears

7 So your <u>icons</u> in the window are as wavy as a souse,
  Ⓐ religious symbols
  Ⓑ graphic symbols
  Ⓒ emblems
  Ⓓ idols

   Advantage Reading Grade 8 © 2005 Creative Teaching Press

Comprehension: **Fact and Opinion**

Have Fun!

A **fact** is a statement that can be proved through research, while an **opinion** is a belief that might be deeply felt, but cannot be proved. For example, it's a fact that the use of computers is increasing worldwide, but it's an opinion that they are more trouble than they are worth. As you read, you must be able to separate facts from opinions and use facts, along with your previous knowledge and your values, to form your own opinions

After reading the poem on page 89, answer questions 1 through 5. They focus on facts and opinions about computers, some relating to the poem and some not.

1 Choose the statement that is a fact.

    Ⓐ The poem doesn't really make sense.
    Ⓑ The stanzas rhyme in an *aabb* pattern.
    Ⓒ The poet knows a lot about computers.
    Ⓓ The poet was upset with his grandsons.

2 Choose the statement that is an opinion.

    Ⓕ Computer functions can be disrupted by electrical surges.
    Ⓖ Expertise with computers can help you get a job.
    Ⓗ Computers are a necessary evil in our lives.
    Ⓙ Computers store data on their hard drives.

3 Choose the statement that is a fact.

    Ⓐ You don't need to know any math if you have a computer.
    Ⓑ It is impossible to get a job without computer expertise.
    Ⓒ Many new appliances have computerized functions.
    Ⓓ Computers are taking over our lives.

4 Write an opinion about computers or this poem.

_____

_____

5 Write a fact about computers or this poem.

_____

_____

Vocabulary: Frequently Misused Words

Have Fun!

The English language contains many homophones—pairs or groups of words that sound alike but have different spellings and meanings. You must be familiar with the meanings of similar words so you can determine which word to use.

Read each sentence and think about the meanings of the words in parentheses. Then underline the correct homophone for that sentence.

1. Did you read the (forward/foreword) to the book?

2. The crowd had become increasingly (hostile/hostel).

3. The runner had only one more barrier to (hurdle/hurtle).

4. She tried to (lesson/lessen) the shock, but I was still stunned.

5. We (least/leased) a car instead of buying it.

6. Toward dawn, when the sky was (lightning/lightening), we found them.

7. The prospector found a forgotten (load/lode) of silver in the old mine.

8. She drew her (mantle/mantel) closer to ward off the cold.

9. The scar was right above his (navel/naval).

10. Ann Chapwood (overseas/oversees) the shipping department.

11. Some doctors do not spend enough time with their (patience/patients).

12. We took a (pole/poll) to see how many liked each topic.

13. The fish was rotting and had begun to (wreak/reek).

14. The farmer demonstrated how to (sheer/shear) a sheep.

15. The river was (teaming/teeming) with trout and other fish.

Advantage Reading Grade 8 © 2005 Creative Teaching Press

Vocabulary: **Content Words**

Have Fun!

Here's your opportunity to add some fun words to your vocabulary. Each word below is probably unfamiliar to you, so it is defined. Your task is to use each word in a sentence. This way, you will begin to incorporate the word into your vocabulary so you can have fun and befuddle your friends.

1 apolaustic: completely devoted to having fun

_____

2 bibliobibuli: someone who reads too much

_____

3 borborygmic: describing the rumbling of one's stomach

_____

4 caseifaction: the act of turning into cheese

_____

5 corrigendum: a mistake, especially in a book

_____

6 discalced: going barefoot

_____

7 eesome: good to look at

_____

8 epeolatry: the worship of words

_____

9 fantods: feeling fidgety

_____

10 flummery: meaningless chatter

_____

The History of Video Games

It's hard to imagine a time before video games, but there was one. The first video game was created way back in 1958. A physicist named William Higinbotham invented a video game that was something like table tennis. His goal was to keep visitors entertained at the Brookhaven National Laboratories, where he worked. This game was played on an oscilloscope, a device that displays an electrical signal. He called the game "Tennis for Two." Higinbotham was not impressed with his invention, however, and did not patent it.

Four years later, Steve Russell, a student at Massachusetts Institute of Technology, invented Spacewar! It was the first video game played on a computer and took him about 200 hours to program. In this two-player game, spaceships fired torpedoes at each other while they tried to avoid the gravitational pull of the sun. By the mid-1960s, every research computer in the nation had a copy of this new game. However, Russell never made a penny from his invention.

In 1967, Ralph Baer, an engineer at a military electronics firm, created the first video game played on a television set. He called it "Chase."

In 1971, Nolan Bushnell and Ted Dabney created a game called Computer Space. It was the first coin-operated arcade game. They built it by turning the bedroom of Bushnell's daughter into a workshop. The game was based on Spacewar!, an invention of their friend Steve Russell. However, people thought Computer Space was too complicated to play, so it was not well accepted.

In 1975, Bushnell and Dabney decided to go into business for themselves and started Atari Computers. Soon after, Bushnell invented a simpler arcade game. He called it Pong because of the noise the ball made when it hit something. Pong was so popular that the test unit became flooded with quarters and broke down!

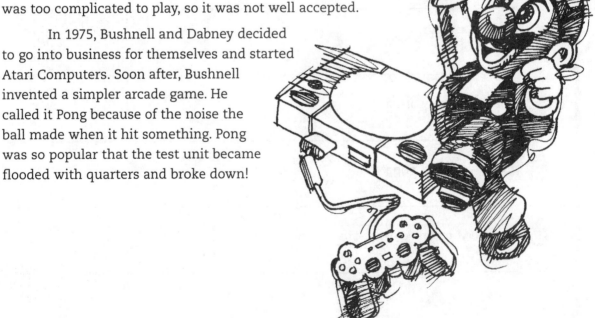

Advantage Reading Grade 8 © 2005 Creative Teaching Press

Then Baer invented a television game system that he called "the Odyssey." It was the first video game that could be played at home. Magnavox sold more than 100,000 units of the Odyssey, which was programmed with 12 games. People bought the Odyssey because they wanted a home version of Pong.

Along with this success came the first concerns about violence in the games. In Death Race 2000, players won points by running over stick figures. When the public objected, the game was taken off the market.

In 1976, Bushnell sold Atari to Warner Communications for $28 million. Two years later, Atari began selling computers. However, customers associated the company with games. They did not buy many Atari computers.

By 1978, Nintendo, a Japanese company, had entered the arcade market. By 1979, Milton Bradley was selling the first programmable, handheld video game. By now, players could insert cartridges into the console to change games and use a new controller called a trackball. They also could control the games better with a keyboard.

As the sales of video games rose, more people became concerned about their violence. In 1993, a rating board was created. Now all game packages suggest the appropriate ages for players and warn about any violent content. As arcades started to offer more "riding" games, such as skiing and snowboarding, these games actually became more popular than the violent games.

PlayStation was introduced in 1994, and people bought 20 million units in its first two years. In 1999, PlayStation 2 sold out the first morning it was introduced. By 2001, games were being sold with built-in hard drives and Ethernet ports.

By now, you probably have seen many more improvements to video games, with many more to come. Just for fun, ask your grandparents what life was like back before video games!

Name _____

Reading: **Comprehension**

After reading the article on pages 94 and 95, answer questions 1 through 5.

1 Which detail from the article shows the popularity of video games?

Ⓐ Bushnell and Dabney began a company they called Atari.

Ⓑ Spacewar! was the first video game played on a computer.

Ⓒ People bought 20 million units of PlayStation in two years.

Ⓓ Bushnell's simpler game was more popular than his first one.

2 Do you think Computer Space would be popular now? Why or why not?

_____

_____

_____

_____

3 Which video game or console was invented first?

Ⓐ Pong

Ⓑ Odyssey

Ⓒ Spacewar!

Ⓓ Computer Space

4 Are you surprised that video games have such a long history? Explain your answer.

_____

_____

_____

_____

5 Which conclusion is accurate, based on this article?

Ⓐ Video games have fascinated people since their invention.

Ⓑ The first video games made their inventors wealthy.

Ⓒ The video game industry started by accident.

Ⓓ Only young people enjoy video games.

Advantage Reading Grade 8 © 2005 Creative Teaching Press

This story, set in the present time, is mostly told in an exchange of E-mail messages, a very contemporary way of communicating. After reading pages 97 through 99, answer the questions on pages 100 and 101. The title, as you may already know, is short for "Correct Me If I'm Wrong."

CMIIW

From: Emily
To: Amanda
Sent: Thursday, January 12, 3:38 PM
Subject: Drats!

My mom still won't get me a cell phone! Can u believe it? What do I have to do to prove I'm super responsible? She won't even get me call waiting so I can tell when someone else wants to talk to me! I mean, I'm in the Dark Ages here, right? UGH!! Call waiting wouldn't help now anyway 'cause my big sister is hogging our only phone line. I mean, really!
BTW, do u want to go out 4 pizza with the rest of us after the BB game Fryday night? Don't say no, again, OK?

From: Amanda
To: Emily
Sent: Thursday, January 12, 5:14 PM
Subject: No phone here either!

My mom's on our phone right now. She says she needs to call my aunt Gail, but why can't she do it while I'm at school? Anyway, I don't know about pizza after the game. Tomorrow night's my first time to be cheerleader, so I might be really tired. I'll probably just head for home after the game. I sure hope the team wins tomorrow. I also hope my cheerleading uniform fits by then. It's a little tight now, but I have a plan. See you at school!

From: Emily
To: Amanda
Sent: Friday, January 13, 3:02 PM
Subject: Where were u?

I saved u a place at lunch, but u never showed up! I looked like a jerk sitting there practically all by myself. Where were u? U weren't skipping lunch again, were u?

From: Amanda
To: Emily
Sent: Friday, January 13, 4:48 PM
Subject: Sorry!

I had to stay in math and take a make-up test at lunchtime. I guess I forgot to tell you in homeroom. I gotta run now—really. I figure if I run down to the gas station and back, I'll fit into my new cheerleading uniform. This better work! TTYL

From: Emily
To: Amanda
Sent: Friday, January 13, 5:07 PM
Subject: OK

OIC! I was the last one out of math class today, but I guess I just didn't see u. BTW, isn't the gas station a couple of miles from your house? Rn't u going to be 2 tired to cheerlead tonight? U are really going to need some pizza afterward. It's not 2 late to say u'll come with us, u know! Say u will, Mandy!

From: Amanda
To: Emily
Sent: Saturday, January 14, 10:32 AM
Subject: Mist U!

Wasn't the game great last night? Go, Warriors, go! Did you see Michael come over and talk to me? I wish I hadn't looked like a sausage stuffed into my uniform. I heard him ask Jill to go get pizza with him afterward, but I can see why he'd like her. She is so skinny! But I don't care. I don't like pizza anyway. What's up with you today?

From: Emily
To: Amanda
Sent: Saturday, January 14, 11:15 AM
Subject: CMIIW

Mandy, are u ok? CMIIW, but u looked a little worn out last night. One time I even thought u were going 2 fall down. I think u would of if Suzanne hadn't caught u. I looked all over the place for u after the game, but I couldn't find u. I wanted to ask u again to come with us for pizza. U need to eat more to fit into your cheerleading uniform! I could see from where I was sitting that it's at least a whole size 2 big for u. I'm coming over after lunch, OK? I'll bring some of my grandma's cookies 'cause they always help me feel better!

Advantage Reading Grade 8 © 2005 Creative Teaching Press

From: Amanda
To: Emily
Sent: Saturday, January 14, 11:20 AM
Subject: Wait!

Em, don't come now! I'm headed out for a run, and I won't be back for a while. Come later, ok?

From: Emily
To: Amanda
Sent: Saturday, January 14, 3:13 PM
Subject: RU OK?

I was just at your house, and your mom said u were taking a nap. She also said u skipped lunch because u didn't feel good. Did u run 2 far this morning? I'm coming over after dinner, and u better b there! I'm getting worried about u!

From: Amanda
To: Emily
Sent: Saturday, January 14, 3:25 AM
Subject: I'm OK

I'll see you after dinner, Em. I'm fine, but I'll be better if you just don't bring any cookies, OK?

Emily sat and stared at her computer screen for a long time before she finally shook her head and went to find her mom. They had a long talk, but today the subject of cell phones never came up. Then Emily and her mom walked over to Amanda's house.

A little later, Amanda was resting in her bedroom—how did she get so tired?—when she heard her mom calling her. She pulled herself off the bed and headed for the kitchen, but when she got there, she blinked in surprise. "Em! Mrs. Mettler! Uh…, hi!" Then she glanced nervously around the kitchen. "Uh, you didn't bring those cookies, did you, Em?"

Amanda's mom pushed her lips tightly together. She looked pale, but determined. "We need to talk about those cookies, Mandy."

Name _____

Reading: Comprehension

After reading CMIIW, answer questions 1 through 10.

1 What is the major conflict in this story?

    Ⓐ Amanda's cheerleading uniform does not fit.

    Ⓑ Emily's parents won't get her a cell phone.

    Ⓒ Amanda thinks she is overweight.

    Ⓓ Amanda is trying to avoid Emily.

2 Which character changes the most in this story? Explain your answer.

_____

_____

_____

_____

3 Why does Amanda have trouble cheerleading at the game?

    Ⓐ Her uniform is too tight.

    Ⓑ She is not eating enough.

    Ⓒ She is distracted by Michael.

    Ⓓ She is still learning the cheers.

4 Why didn't Emily see Amanda in the math classroom after class was over?

_____

_____

_____

_____

5 Why does Amanda think Michael likes Jill?

    Ⓐ She thinks Jill is a better cheerleader.

    Ⓑ She thinks Jill is more popular.

    Ⓒ She thinks Jill is prettier.

    Ⓓ She thinks Jill is thinner.

Reading: Comprehension

6 Why does Amanda tell Emily not to bring over any cookies?

Ⓕ Amanda doesn't feel well, and eating might make her worse.

Ⓖ She does not like that kind of cookies.

Ⓗ She is afraid she will eat them.

Ⓙ She just isn't hungry.

7 How can you tell that Amanda is not being realistic about how much she weighs?

_____

_____

_____

_____

8 What does Amanda seem to be telling herself?

Ⓕ If she exercises enough, she'll be a good cheerleader.

Ⓖ If she doesn't eat any pizza, her uniform will fit.

Ⓗ If she gets thin enough, everything will be fine.

Ⓙ If she doesn't eat any cookies, she'll feel better.

9 What are three of the clues that Amanda is in trouble?

_____

_____

_____

_____

10 What is the climax of this short story?

Ⓕ Amanda tells Emily she can come over.

Ⓖ Emily tells her mom about Amanda.

Ⓗ Emily decides to help her friend.

Ⓙ Amanda decides to start eating.

Graphic Information: **Double-Bar Graphs**

Have Fun!

⭐ Which age and gender groups use the Internet for entertainment the most often? A study in Brazil surveyed about 1,100 home Internet users to find out. Of those in the survey, 40 percent used the Internet for entertainment and 73 percent used it to gather information. About 32 percent said they used the Internet for entertainment and information.

The top graph shows an analysis of the 40 percent (about 440 people) who used the Internet for entertainment. The bottom graph displays results for the 73 percent (about 800 people) who used it for information. Notice that each double bar shows the results for males and for females. After studying the graphs, answer the questions on page 102.

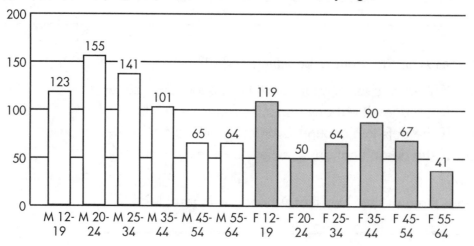

Using the Internet for Entertainment, by Age/Sex

source: TGI Brasil, IBOPE

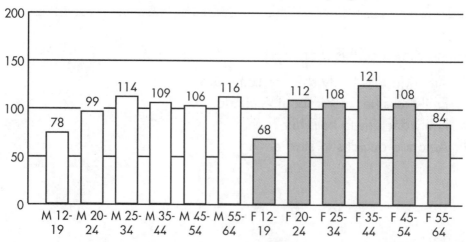

Using the Internet for Information, by Age/Sex

source: TGI Brasil, IBOPE

Reading: **Comprehension**

After studying the double-bar graphs on page 102, answer questions 1 through 5.

1 Which conclusion is accurate, based on the Internet for Entertainment graph?

    Ⓐ Use by men and women is basically equal across the age groups.

    Ⓑ More young men than young women use the Internet for entertainment.

    Ⓒ Many more older men than older women use the Internet for entertainment.

    Ⓓ Male teenagers use the Internet for entertainment more than any other group.

2 Describe the pattern shown for males using the Internet for Entertainment.

_____

_____

3 Which conclusion is accurate, based on the Internet for Information graph?

    Ⓐ Use by men and women is basically equal across the age groups.

    Ⓑ More young women than young men use the Internet for information.

    Ⓒ Many more older women than older men use the Internet for information.

    Ⓓ Teenagers use the Internet for information more than any other age group.

4 Describe the pattern shown for females using the Internet for Information.

_____

_____

5 Which statement is a fact, supported by the patterns shown on the graphs?

    Ⓐ Use for entertainment is influenced more by the user's age than use for information.

    Ⓑ Older people avoid the Internet because they are uncomfortable with computers.

    Ⓒ Teenagers waste a lot of their time using the Internet for entertainment.

    Ⓓ The use of the Internet for entertainment is rising rapidly.

Have Fun!

Writing: Narrative

★ Narrative writing tells a story, which might be fiction or nonfiction. The purpose is to entertain, and the form might be a personal story, poem, play, eyewitness account, biography, fable, or myth. In a narrative, something happens; usually the main character solves a problem.

Here is your chance to write a narrative. First, you must choose a type of narrative and the main idea. If you are going to write a personal story, you might focus on a time when you thought you were treated unfairly, but then you found out you were mistaken. Or you could write about someone who has to be brave for some reason. You have endless possibilities. The graphic organizer below can help with your planning.

Characters
Setting
Problem/Challenge/Complication
Attempts to Solve It
Final Resolution or Climax
Conclusion

Advantage Reading Grade 8 © 2005 Creative Teaching Press

Have Fun!

Writing: Narrative

Now write the first draft of your narrative, using additional paper, if needed. Follow your organizer on page 104. If you are writing a story, you can indicate the personality and values of your characters by what they say, what they do, and how other people react to them. Be sure to include lots of dialogue and try to build suspense as the characters try to solve the problem they face. Don't forget to think of an interesting title for your narrative.

_____

_____

_____

_____

_____

_____

_____

_____

_____

_____

_____

_____

_____

After you finish your first draft, look for ways to make it clearer, more interesting, and better organized. Ask a friend or family member to read it and suggest improvements. For example, do each character's actions make sense?

Have Fun!

Writing: **Narrative**

⭐ Now write the final draft of your narrative, using additional sheets of paper, if necessary. Consider your partner's editing suggestions and avoid errors in spelling, punctuation, grammar, and word usage. You might illustrate your narrative with one or more drawings.

_____

_____

_____

_____

_____

_____

_____

_____

_____

_____

_____

_____

_____

_____

_____

_____

Fun for Free

Make a list of free (or almost free) ways to have fun at your school and in your community. For example, your community library might offer environmental or writers groups just for teenagers. You might be able to take skateboarding lessons, swim, or practice your free throws at a community center. Your school might sponsor clubs, teams, or special-interest groups that you could join. Find ways to help other students at your school learn more about these opportunities.

More Fun Words

If you enjoyed using the words on page 93, you can find more fun words at this Web site: *http://rinkworks.com/words/funwords.shtml*. This site also has other fun information, such as lists of palindromes (sentences that read the same backward and forward) and contronyms (words that are their own antonyms).

Find out More about Eating Disorders

The story on pages 97–99 focuses on a serious problem for young people: eating disorders. You may know someone who is mistakenly convinced that he or she is overweight and is willing to do anything to be thinner. Understanding this problem is the first step in helping. You can learn more by visiting the Web site for the National Eating Disorders Look under General Information for the sec and/or students.

Check out these books.

Game Programming for Teens by Maneesh Sethi (Premier Press)

Inventing Toys: Kids Having Fun Learning Science by Ed Sobey (Zephyr Press)

The Ultimate History of Video Games: From Pong to Pokemon—The Story Behind the Craze That Touched Our Lives and Changed the World by Steven L. Kent (Prima Lifestyles)

Page 5
Students should list thoughtful comments in each column of the chart.

Page 6
1   A
2   G
3   A
4   G
5   B
6   G

Page 7
1   B
2   J
3   D
4   J
5   C
6   G
7   B
8   H

Page 9
1   A
2   G
3   A
4   Sample answers: Global warming is a dire threat to our environment; it is the biggest problem humanity has faced; it is the invention of tree-huggers.
5   Sample answers: It is an issue that concerns many people; people have different opinions about the existence of global warming and about its effects.

Page 10
1   D
2   H
3   C
4   G
5   B

Page 11
1   barren
2   adverse
3   annual
4   appraise
5   casual
6   collision
7   contiguous
8   commended
9   dissent
10   depositions
11   deference
12   Irascible
13   indignant
14   expand
15   emerge

Page 12
1   B
2   G
3   A
4   J
5   C
6   F
7   C
8   F

Page 14
1   A
2   G
3   A
4   Sample answer: To point out that drastic climate changes have occurred in the past without human interference.
5   D

Page 16
1   B
2   The permafrost is melting now due to rising temperatures.
3   B
4   Warmer temperatures are melting the ice.
5   D

Page 18
1   A
2   No. You should realize that a few warm hours do not indicate a trend.
3   A
4   Answers will vary. You may write that some people do not know any other way to get others to do what they want.
5   B

Page 20
1   B
2   H
3   Sample answer: Both graphs show a cooler climate until about 1910–1920, then a slightly warmer climate, followed by a cooling off in the 1960s–1970s, and another rise after 1980. However, the changes are more extreme on the U.S. map until 1980, when the global climate becomes even warmer than the U.S. climate.
4   G
5   Answers may vary. Sample answer: The graph will show that the climate remains warmer than usual, about the same as from 1980–2000. As sources of pollution increase in the United States, people are becoming more aware of the problem and putting laws in place to reduce the pollution that leads to global warming.

Pages 21–23
Your myth should explain a natural phenomenon or other event related to global warming. The plot should make sense as a myth and be clearly written.

Page 25
You might include words such as monarchy, taxation, patriots, colonies, freedom, George Washington, and so on.

Page 26

1 A
2 G
3 D
4 F
5 D
6 H

Page 27

1 For example, For instance
2 Still, Yet, Nevertheless, However
3 but
4 Consequently, Therefore
5 In addition, Also
6 Then, Next, Afterward
7 because
8 Now

Page 29

1 B
2 Sample answer: Paine was referring to soldiers who fight only when weather is pleasant and they are likely to win.
3 A
4 Possible answer: Paine writes that this situation will be challenging (try men's souls). He says some will turn away from the fight (shrink from service). He says the conflict will be hard and victory will not be cheap.
5 B

Page 30

1 B
2 F
3 D
4 F
5 B
6 F

Page 31

1 ails
2 boring
3 boulder
4 borne
5 bough
6 bridle

7 broach
8 callous
9 canvass
10 castes
11 censor
12 serial
13 course
14 Corps
15 islet

Page 32

1 A
2 J
3 D
4 G
5 C
6 J
7 D
8 G

Page 35–36

1 D
2 Possible answer: No. It appears that he succeeded only as a writer.
3 C
4 There were many fewer people in our nation back then. Half a million people back then was a much higher percentage of the population than half a million people today.
5 C
6 Possible answer: His strong opinions apparently kept people from becoming his friends and supporting him. His drinking probably did not help either.
7 C
8 Answers will vary. You might believe that Paine would be able to sway opinions, as he did long ago. Others might write that we have many more people trying to influence us today and much faster communication, so one person would not have much influence.
9 D

Page 38

1 C
2 G
3 A British patrol had captured him, and he was lucky they let him go, even though they kept his horse.
4 G
5 Sample answer: A young girl is forbidden by her father to ride to Lexington to fight the British soldiers, but she unknowingly helps Paul Revere get there.

Page 40

1 B
2 Possible answer: They both were patriots, both helped warn the colonists that the British were coming, and both were caught by a British patrol. However, they took different routes that night. Paul Revere is better known by far and was held longer by the British patrol that night, while Dawes managed to escape.
3 C
4 Answers will vary. You might note that many people know about Paul Revere's ride from the poem by Longfellow, which does not mention any other riders.
5 C

Pages 41–43

Your report should relate directly to the American Revolution, be clear and well organized, and contain three to five main points. It should begin with an interesting title and an introduction and close with a conclusion.

Page 45

You should provide thoughtful, logical answers to the questions.

Page 46

1. neophyte
2. eulogy
3. excursion
4. optimal
5. administer
6. inhibit
7. analysis
8. plurality
9. monogamy

Page 47

1. C
2. H
3. A
4. G
5. A
6. H
7. D
8. H

Page 49

1. C
2. J
3. D
4. H

Page 50

1. phase
2. your
3. guilt
4. disburse
5. complements
6. whether
7. peers
8. may be
9. prey
10. kernel
11. pedal
12. Their
13. vile
14. principal
15. straight

Page 51

1. accommodate
2. acknowledgment
3. amateur
4. assistance
5. cemetery
6. conscientious
7. eligible
8. environment
9. exceed
10. exaggerate
11. extraordinary
12. hindrance
13. irrelevant
14. preferred
15. privilege

Page 52

1. D
2. G
3. C
4. G
5. B
6. H
7. D
8. H

Page 55

1. B
2. G
3. B
4. Possible summary: Technology developed for the space program is being applied in many ways on Earth, justifying the cost of the space program.
5. Towns can use this natural, inexpensive way to purify their water.

Pages 58–59

1. C
2. geek
3. B
4. H
5. D
6. Answers will vary. You might predict that the girls will still be friends because they seem to like each other. Others may think that Jill does not share Susan's interest in robots, and so they may drift apart.

7. C
8. J
9. Answers will vary. You might think that the boys would realize that Susan could still help them with their robot. Others might think that the boys would be convinced that Susan (and all other girls) know nothing about robots and reject any further help from her.

Page 61

1. D
2. C6
3. A
4. Enter the equal sign in a cell. Then enter the larger number (or the name of its cell), the minus sign (-), and the smaller number (or the name of its cell). Press enter.
5. A

Page 62–64

Your directions should be clear and in chronological order. Each step should be numbered and start with a verb. The instructions should have an informative title and an introduction that orients the reader to what is coming.

Page 66

Your paragraph will vary, but it should contain clear, thoughtful responses to several of the questions.

Page 67

1. permeates
2. contraband
3. malevolent
4. euphemism
5. heptarchy
6. pericardium
7. extraneous
8. countermands

Advantage Reading Grade 8 © 2005 Creative Teaching Press

Page 68

1. A
2. F
3. C
4. G
5. D
6. G
7. C
8. H

Pages 70

1. A
2. Answers may vary. You might predict that Bonnie will tire of Alice's manipulation, but others will probably predict that these two people like each other and want the best for each other, so they will remain friends.
3. D
4. Answers will vary, but you might predict that Bonnie will be chosen for the swim team, mostly because Alice says Bonnie is cut out to be a swimmer.

Pages 71

1. A
2. F
3. D
4. H
5. C
6. H
7. C
8. F

Page 72

1. session
2. cord
3. clique
4. symbol
5. dual
6. fainted
7. fare
8. fined
9. flair
10. hail
11. hanger
12. hoard
13. incite
14. insure
15. lien

Page 73

1. A
2. G
3. A
4. G
5. D
6. J
7. D
8. G

Page 76

1. D
2. Possible answers: to improve their overall athletic ability; to add variety to their workouts
3. D
4. Answers will vary, but you might mention an interest in several sports or a need for variety. You might also express a firm belief in training only for the sport they play.
5. D

Pages 79

1. C
2. Answers will vary. Here are some possibilities: he had seen, heard, or read about that kind of cream before; the tube did not have a label, which was unusual; Tyler was too quick to defend his use of the cream.
3. B
4. Ty has failed to keep the coach's trust.
5. D

Page 81

1. C
2. The percentages in each graph do not add up to 100.
3. A
4. G
5. Answers will vary, but you should explain whether you agree with the findings in each bar graph.

Page 82–84

For your biography, you should choose someone who is related to health or sports. Your biography should present a coherent picture of the person's life, covering most or all of the topics in the graphic organizer on page 82, and make it clear why you chose to write about that person.

Page 86

Your responses to the questions should be clear and thoughtful.

Page 87

1. D
2. F
3. D
4. G
5. D

Page 88

1. B
2. G
3. B
4. J
5. C
6. J

Page 90

1. A
2. G
3. D
4. G
5. D
6. J
7. B

Page 91

1. B
2. H
3. C
4. Possible opinions: Computers are the greatest thing ever invented; life was better without computers; this poem is fun to read.
5. Possible facts: Most businesses rely on computers; Gene Ziegler wrote this poem.

Page 92

1 foreword
2 hostile
3 hurdle
4 lessen
5 leased
6 lightening
7 lode
8 mantel
9 navel
10 oversees
11 patients
12 poll
13 reek
14 shear
15 teeming

Page 93

Your sentence should use each word in a way that corresponds to its given meaning.

Page 96

1 C
2 Answers will vary, as you may think players are eager for complex games now, but others might think that what was challenging back in 1971 would be boring now.
3 C
4 Answers will vary. You might have assumed that video games were brand new since they are so popular with young people, while others might understand that these complex devices took a long time to develop.
5 A

Pages 100–101

1 C
2 Emily changes the most because she stops worrying about getting a cell phone and starts worrying about more important things, especially her friend's well-being.
3 B
4 Amanda wasn't there. She said she was taking a make-up test as an excuse for skipping lunch.
5 D
6 H
7 Amanda says she looks like a sausage stuffed into her cheerleading uniform, but Emily says the uniform is too big for her.
8 H
9 Possible clues: she is not eating, exercising a lot, thinking about her weight all the time, not being realistic about her weight, getting weak from not eating, avoiding activities that involve food, and so on.
10 H

Page 103

1 B
2 Sample answer: Male use is high for the 12–19 age group, increases for the 20–24 group, and then drops, leveling off for men aged 45 and older.
3 A
4 Sample answer: Female use is lowest for the 12–19 age group, increases and stays at about the same level for the next four age groups, and then drops slightly for the 55–64 group.
5 A

Pages 104–106

Your narrative should be clear and well organized, based on a problem that characters face and resolve.

Advantage Reading Grade 8 © 2005 Creative Teaching Press